# MATH
# WEEKLY
# PRACTICE
## Grade 2

Credits
Authors: Kayleigh Heubel and Rachel Jacobs
Copy Editor: Jennifer B. Stith

Visit *carsondellosa.com* for correlations to Common Core, state, national, and Canadian provincial standards.

Carson-Dellosa Publishing, LLC
PO Box 35665
Greensboro, NC 27425 USA
carsondellosa.com

978-1-4838-2796-4
01-053167784

# Table of Contents

# Introduction

The Weekly Practice series provides 40 weeks of essential daily practice in either math or language arts. It is the perfect supplement to any classroom curriculum and provides standards-based activities for every day of the week but Friday.

The activities are intended as homework assignments for Monday through Thursday and cover a wide spectrum of standards-based skills. The skills are presented at random to provide comprehensive learning but are repeated systematically throughout the book. The intention is to offer regular, focused practice to ensure mastery and retention.

Each 192-page book provides 40 weeks of reproducible pages, a standards alignment matrix, flash cards, and an answer key. The reproducible pages are perfect for homework but also work well for morning work, early finishers, and warm-up activities.

# About This Book

Each page contains a variety of short, fun exercises that build in difficulty across the span of the book. The activities are divided into two sections:

• The Daily Extension Activities at the front of the book are intended to engage both student and family. These off-the-page activities are simple and fun so that students will look forward to this practice time at home. The activities span one week at a time. The instructions are clear and simple so that students can follow them with or without assistance in their homes. None need be returned to school.

• The daily practice section involves more comprehensive learning. Because of the simplicity of directions and straightforward tasks, students will be able to complete most tasks independently in a short period of time. There are four pages of activities per week, allowing for testing or a student break on Friday if desired. These pages are intended to be brought back to school.

Pages can be offered in any order, making it possible to reinforce specific skills when needed. However, skills are repeated regularly throughout the book to ensure retention over time, making a strong case for using pages sequentially.

An answer key is included for the daily practice section. You can check answers as a group for a quick follow-up lesson or monitor students' progress individually. Follow the basic page layout provided at the beginning of the answer key to match answers to page placement. Also included in the book is a set of flash cards. Reproduce them to give to students for at-home practice, or place them in classroom centers.

# Common Core State Standards
## Alignment Matrix

| Standards | W1 | W2 | W3 | W4 | W5 | W6 | W7 | W8 | W9 | W10 | W11 | W12 | W13 | W14 | W15 | W16 | W17 | W18 | W19 | W20 |
|---|---|---|---|---|---|---|---|---|---|---|---|---|---|---|---|---|---|---|---|---|
| 2.OA.A.1 | • | • | • | • | • | • | • | • | • | • | • | • | • | • | • | • | • | • | • | • |
| 2.OA.B.2 | • | • | • | • | • | • | • | • |  | • | • |  | • |  | • | • |  | • | • | • |
| 2.OA.C.3 | • | • | • | • | • | • | • |  | • | • | • |  | • |  | • |  | • | • |  | • |
| 2.OA.C.4 | • | • | • | • |  | • |  | • | • |  | • | • | • | • | • | • |  | • | • | • |
| 2.NBT.A.1 | • | • | • | • | • | • | • | • | • | • | • | • | • | • | • | • | • |  | • | • |
| 2.NBT.A.2 | • | • | • | • | • | • |  | • | • | • | • | • | • |  | • |  | • |  | • | • |
| 2.NBT.A.3 | • | • | • | • |  | • | • | • | • | • | • |  | • |  | • |  | • | • |  | • |
| 2.NBT.A.4 | • | • | • | • | • |  |  | • | • | • |  | • | • |  | • | • | • | • | • | • |
| 2.NBT.B.5 | • | • | • | • | • | • |  | • | • |  | • | • | • |  | • |  | • |  | • | • |
| 2.NBT.B.6 |  |  | • |  | • | • |  | • |  | • | • |  | • |  | • |  | • |  | • | • |
| 2.NBT.B.7 | • | • | • | • |  | • | • | • | • |  | • | • | • |  | • |  | • |  | • | • |
| 2.NBT.B.8 | • | • |  |  | • | • | • |  | • | • | • |  | • |  | • | • |  | • |  | • |
| 2.NBT.B.9 |  |  |  |  | • |  |  |  |  |  |  |  |  |  | • |  |  |  |  |  |
| 2.MD.A.1 | • |  | • | • | • | • | • | • | • |  | • |  | • | • | • |  | • |  | • | • |
| 2.MD.A.2 |  | • |  |  | • | • |  |  | • |  | • | • |  | • |  |  |  | • | • |  |
| 2.MD.A.3 |  |  | • |  |  | • |  | • |  |  | • |  |  |  | • |  |  | • |  |  |
| 2.MD.A.4 |  |  | • |  |  |  | • |  | • |  | • | • |  | • |  |  |  | • |  | • |
| 2.MD.B.5 |  |  |  | • |  | • |  |  | • |  | • |  | • |  | • | • |  | • |  |  |
| 2.MD.B.6 |  |  | • |  | • |  | • |  | • |  | • |  | • |  | • |  | • |  | • | • |
| 2.MD.C.7 | • | • |  | • | • |  | • | • |  | • | • | • | • | • | • | • | • | • | • | • |
| 2.MD.C.8 | • | • | • | • | • | • | • | • | • |  | • | • | • | • | • | • | • | • | • | • |
| 2.MD.D.9 |  |  |  | • |  |  |  | • |  | • |  |  | • |  |  |  | • | • |  | • |
| 2.MD.D.10 |  | • | • | • | • |  | • |  | • |  | • | • | • | • | • | • |  | • | • | • |
| 2.G.A.1 | • | • | • |  |  |  | • | • |  | • | • | • | • | • | • | • | • |  | • | • |
| 2.G.A.2 | • |  | • |  | • |  | • |  | • | • | • |  |  | • |  |  | • |  |  | • |
| 2.G.A.3 | • | • |  | • | • |  | • |  |  |  | • |  | • | • | • | • |  | • | • |  |

W = Week

# Common Core State Standards
## Alignment Matrix

| Standards | W21 | W22 | W23 | W24 | W25 | W26 | W27 | W28 | W29 | W30 | W31 | W32 | W33 | W34 | W35 | W36 | W37 | W38 | W39 | W40 |
|---|---|---|---|---|---|---|---|---|---|---|---|---|---|---|---|---|---|---|---|---|
| 2.OA.A.1 | ● | ● | ● | ● | ● | ● | ● | ● | ● | ● | ● | ● | ● | ● | ● | ● | ● | ● | ● | ● |
| 2.OA.B.2 | ● | ● | ● | ● | ● | ● | ● | ● | ● | ● | ● | ● | ● | ● | ● | ● | ● | ● | ● | ● |
| 2.OA.C.3 | ● | ● | ● | ● | ● | ● | ● | ● | ● | ● | ● | ● |  |  |  | ● | ● |  | ● | ● |
| 2.OA.C.4 |  | ● | ● |  |  | ● |  |  |  |  | ● | ● |  | ● | ● | ● | ● |  |  |  |
| 2.NBT.A.1 | ● | ● | ● | ● | ● | ● | ● | ● | ● | ● | ● | ● | ● | ● | ● | ● | ● | ● | ● | ● |
| 2.NBT.A.2 | ● | ● | ● | ● | ● | ● | ● | ● | ● | ● | ● | ● | ● | ● | ● | ● | ● | ● |  | ● |
| 2.NBT.A.3 | ● | ● | ● | ● | ● | ● |  | ● | ● | ● |  | ● | ● | ● | ● | ● | ● |  |  | ● |
| 2.NBT.A.4 | ● | ● | ● | ● |  | ● |  | ● | ● | ● | ● | ● | ● | ● | ● | ● |  | ● | ● | ● |
| 2.NBT.B.5 | ● | ● | ● | ● | ● | ● | ● | ● | ● | ● | ● | ● | ● |  |  |  |  | ● | ● | ● |
| 2.NBT.B.6 | ● |  | ● | ● |  | ● | ● |  | ● | ● |  | ● | ● | ● |  |  |  |  |  |  |
| 2.NBT.B.7 |  | ● |  | ● | ● |  | ● |  |  |  | ● |  |  | ● |  |  |  |  |  |  |
| 2.NBT.B.8 | ● | ● | ● | ● | ● |  | ● | ● | ● | ● | ● | ● | ● |  |  | ● | ● | ● | ● |  |
| 2.NBT.B.9 |  |  |  | ● |  |  |  |  |  | ● |  | ● |  |  |  |  |  |  |  |  |
| 2.MD.A.1 |  | ● | ● | ● | ● | ● |  | ● | ● | ● |  | ● |  |  |  |  | ● |  | ● |  |
| 2.MD.A.2 | ● |  | ● |  | ● |  |  |  | ● | ● |  |  |  |  | ● | ● |  | ● |  | ● |
| 2.MD.A.3 |  | ● |  |  |  |  | ● |  | ● |  | ● | ● | ● | ● | ● |  | ● | ● |  | ● |
| 2.MD.A.4 |  | ● |  | ● |  | ● |  | ● | ● | ● |  |  |  | ● | ● |  |  |  | ● |
| 2.MD.B.5 |  |  | ● |  | ● | ● |  | ● |  |  |  | ● |  |  |  | ● | ● | ● |  |
| 2.MD.B.6 |  | ● |  | ● | ● |  | ● |  | ● | ● | ● |  | ● |  |  | ● | ● |  | ● |  |
| 2.MD.C.7 | ● | ● | ● | ● | ● | ● |  | ● | ● | ● | ● | ● | ● | ● | ● | ● |  |  | ● | ● |
| 2.MD.C.8 | ● | ● | ● | ● | ● | ● | ● | ● | ● | ● | ● | ● | ● | ● | ● | ● | ● | ● | ● | ● |
| 2.MD.D.9 | ● |  |  |  | ● |  | ● | ● |  |  | ● | ● |  |  | ● |  |  | ● |  |  |
| 2.MD.D.10 | ● |  | ● | ● | ● |  | ● | ● | ● |  | ● | ● | ● | ● |  | ● |  | ● | ● |  |
| 2.G.A.1 | ● | ● | ● |  |  | ● | ● | ● | ● | ● | ● | ● |  | ● |  |  | ● | ● | ● | ● |
| 2.G.A.2 |  | ● |  | ● | ● |  | ● | ● | ● | ● |  | ● |  |  | ● | ● | ● | ● | ● | ● |
| 2.G.A.3 | ● | ● | ● |  | ● |  | ● |  | ● | ● | ● | ● |  | ● | ● | ● | ● |  | ● |  |

W = Week

# School to Home Communication

The research is clear that family involvement is strongly linked to student success. Support for student learning at home improves student achievement in school. Educators should not underestimate the significance of this connection.

The activities in this book create an opportunity to create or improve this school-to-home link. The activities span a week at a time and can be sent home as a week-long homework packet each Monday. Simply clip together the strip of fun activities from the front of the book with the pages for Days 1 to 4 for the correct week.

Most of the activities can be completed independently, but many encourage feedback or interaction with a family member. The activities are simple and fun, aiming to create a brief pocket of learning that is enjoyable to all.

In order to make the school-to-home program work for students and their families, we encourage you to reach out to them with an introductory letter. Explain the program and its intent and ask them to partner with you in their children's educational process. Describe the role you expect them to play. Encourage them to offer suggestions or feedback along the way.

A sample letter is included below. Use it as is or create your own letter to introduce this project and elicit their collaboration.

---

Dear Families,

I anticipate a productive and exciting year of learning and look forward to working with you and your child. We have a lot of work to do! I hope we—teacher, student, and family—can work together as a team to achieve the goal of academic progress we all hope for this year.

I will send home a packet of homework each week on _____. There will be two items to complete each day: a single task on a strip plus a full page of focused practice. Each page or strip is labeled Day 1 (for Monday), Day 2, Day 3, or Day 4. There is no homework on Friday.

Please make sure that your student brings back the completed work _____. It is important that these are brought in on time as we may work on some of the lessons as a class.

If you have any questions about this program or would like to talk to me about it, please feel free to call or email me. Thank you for joining me in making this the best year ever for your student!

Sincerely,

_____

_____

_____

---

| | Day 1 | Day 2 | Day 3 | Day 4 |
|---|---|---|---|---|
| **Week 1** | Look around your home. See if you can find at least one object that is a triangle and one that is a trapezoid. | Ask your friends and family members what their favorite snacks are. Record their answers in a tally chart. | Put a handful of coins into a paper bag. Pull out three coins at a time and add them together. | Think: What objects in my home could I count with tens rods? Are there any I would need hundreds blocks to count? |

| | Day 1 | Day 2 | Day 3 | Day 4 |
|---|---|---|---|---|
| **Week 2** | Fill a small cup with candies, peanuts, or other small food. Estimate the number of items in the cup. Then count them. | Count your shoes. Do you have an odd number or an even number? Why do you think that is? | Count the number of spoons and forks you have. Which one do you have more of? How many more? | Find a bookshelf in your home, your classroom, or a library. Count the items on two different shelves. Which shelf has more? |

| | Day 1 | Day 2 | Day 3 | Day 4 |
|---|---|---|---|---|
| **Week 3** | Practice counting from 0 to 100 by 1s, 5s, 10s, and 100s. Which way has the most numbers? The least? | Take a sheet of paper. Fold it so that when you open it, the crease divides it into equal parts. | Count the number of chairs and tables in your home. How many more chairs than tables are there? | Think of as many things as you can that are cones. Then, look around your home to see if you can find any of them. |

| | Day 1 | Day 2 | Day 3 | Day 4 |
|---|---|---|---|---|
| **Week 4** | Count the number of windows in your home. Count the number of lightbulbs. Which number is greater? | Create your own hundreds chart puzzle. See if a family member or friend can solve it. | Number index cards from 1 to 10. Pick two at a time. Write the fact family for the pair of numbers. | Write three numbers that have the digit 1, but in different place values. |

| | Day 1 | Day 2 | Day 3 | Day 4 |
|---|---|---|---|---|
| **Week 5** | Draw a kind of transportation using only geometric shapes. List the shapes you use. | Find five cylinders at your home. What kinds of objects are cylinders? | Take two sheets of paper. Fold one in half lengthwise and one widthwise. Even though they look different, the halves are the same size! | Look around the kitchen. What foods are sold in even numbers that you could write a doubles fact for? Try to find at least three. |

| | Day 1 | Day 2 | Day 3 | Day 4 |
|---|---|---|---|---|
| **Week 6** | Ask your friends and family members in what month they were born. Record the answers in a tally chart. | Look at a pair of dice. How many faces, edges, and vertices does one die have? How many do the dice have in all? | Look for quadrilaterals in your home. Try to find one of each: square, rectangle, and trapezoid. | Think of a number between 1 and 1,000. Have someone try to guess the number using greater than/less than questions. |

| | Day 1 | Day 2 | Day 3 | Day 4 |
|---|---|---|---|---|
| **Week 7** | Count your own change, or borrow some from an adult. How many cents do you have? | Ask your friends or family members what their favorite drinks are. Record their answers on a tally chart. Make a bar graph to show the data. | Make a set of cards with the numbers 1 through 20. Pick two at a time and add the numbers using mental math. | Look for objects with six sides. Are the objects mostly regular hexagons or another kind of irregular hexagon? |

| | Day 1 | Day 2 | Day 3 | Day 4 |
|---|---|---|---|---|
| **Week 8** | Count how many rooms and how many doors your home has. Which does it have more of? How many more? | Estimate the number of foot lengths it would take to cross a room. Then, walk across the room to check your estimate. | Count the pages of two picture books. Write a number sentence to find out how many more pages the longer book has. | Take all of the face cards and jokers out of a deck of cards. Pick two cards at a time and add them together. (Aces = 1) |

| | Day 1 | Day 2 | Day 3 | Day 4 |
|---|---|---|---|---|
| **Week 9** | Write doubles facts for five things you have equal sets of, such as shoes, socks, fingers, etc. | Find a food item that is rectangular, such as a cake or a slice of cheese. Draw different ways to divide it into equal parts. | Look at a price tag. How many dollars and cents are listed? Draw three ways to make the number of cents with coins. | Use equal-length objects, such as pretzel sticks or cotton swabs, to practice making basic shapes with equal side lengths. |

| | Day 1 | Day 2 | Day 3 | Day 4 |
|---|---|---|---|---|
| **Week 10** | Count out 100 pieces of cereal. Practice grouping them by 2s, 5s, and 10s. | Find at least three objects that are spheres. Write the objects' names in a list. | Count the number of digital and analog clocks at your home. Which one do you have more of? How many more? | Ask your family members and friends their favorite colors. Record their answers on a tally chart. Make a bar graph to show the data. |

| | Day 1 | Day 2 | Day 3 | Day 4 |
|---|---|---|---|---|
| **Week 11** | Look for arrays at home. Hint: think of things in equal rows, such as tiles or windowpanes. | Count the number of long-sleeve and short-sleeve shirts you have. Which number is greater? How much greater? | Look at the mirrors in your home. How many are square? Circular? Rectangular? Another shape? | Count the number of people who live in your home. Is it even or odd? |

| | Day 1 | Day 2 | Day 3 | Day 4 |
|---|---|---|---|---|
| **Week 12** | Practice skip counting by 5s, 10s, or 100s as you walk up a set of stairs. Then, skip count backwards on your way down. | Measure the hands on an analog clock. How much longer is the long hand than the short hand to the nearest inch? | Make a set of cards for the numbers 1 through 10. Pick one number at a time and say the doubles fact for that number. (For example, 2: 2 + 2 = 4) | Have a friend or family member draw rectangles on a dot grid or graph paper. Divide the rectangles into equal parts. |

| | Day 1 | Day 2 | Day 3 | Day 4 |
|---|---|---|---|---|
| **Week 13** | Think about your room. How many walls (sides) and corners (angles) does it have? What shape is the room? | Find two books of different sizes. Measure the height of each book. How much taller is the larger book? | Grab a handful of raisins, nuts, or other small snack item. Before eating them, arrange the pieces in an array. | Remove the face cards and Jokers from a deck of cards. Pick two cards at a time and write a subtraction sentence for them. (Aces = 1) |

| | Day 1 | Day 2 | Day 3 | Day 4 |
|---|---|---|---|---|
| **Week 14** | Draw a tic-tac-toe board. Write an addition number sentence for the array that the squares make. Then, play tic-tac-toe with a friend. | Measure the length of your leg and the length of your arm. Which one is longer and by how much? | Ask your friends and family members what are their favorite sports. Record their answers in a tally chart. Make a pictograph to show the data. | Use a paper clip to measure items in your home. Then, use a ruler with in. or cm. How different are your measurements? Explain. |

| | Day 1 | Day 2 | Day 3 | Day 4 |
|---|---|---|---|---|
| **Week 15** | Measure one fork, one spoon, and one knife in in. or cm. Which is the longest? The shortest? | Look at the tables in your home. How many are squares, circles, or rectangles? Are any of them other shapes? | Practice counting time. Starting with an hour (e.g. 5:00), count by groups of five minutes to the next hour. | Use a pie or a pizza (or draw a picture of one) to show how you could cut a circle into halves, thirds, or fourths. |

| | Day 1 | Day 2 | Day 3 | Day 4 |
|---|---|---|---|---|
| **Week 16** | Measure the lengths of several carrots or bananas to the nearest inch. Make a line plot with the measurements. | Write 25 addition problems on a bingo card. Have a friend read the sums until you can call, "Bingo!" | Find the time to the nearest five minutes on an analog clock. Write how it would look on a digital clock. | Make your own addition number search for a sum between 10 and 20. Have an adult or a friend solve your puzzle. |

**10**

| | **Day 1** | **Day 2** | **Day 3** | **Day 4** |
|---|---|---|---|---|
| **Week 17** | Use pieces of cereal or other counters to practice adding two or more two-digit numbers together. (e.g. 35 + 19 + 23; 11 + 28) | 100¢ is the same as $1. Draw at least five ways to make $1 with quarters, dimes, nickels, and pennies. | Estimate the width of a window in in.. Then measure the window. How close was your estimate? | Find a digital clock in your home. Draw what it would look like on an analog clock, to the nearest five minutes. |
| **Week 18** | Take square pieces of sandwich bread. Think of different ways to cut them into halves or fourths. | Make an even group of objects. Divide it into two equal groups. Then divide it into an even group and an odd group. | Take 25 cards from a deck of playing cards. Arrange the cards in as many arrays as you can think of. | Make one list of animals you would measure in cm, and another list of animals you would measure in meters. |
| **Week 19** | Number index cards from 1 to 9. Pick three at a time to make three-digit numbers. Practice adding the three-digit numbers. | Roll a die 15 times. Record how often you roll each number on a line plot. | What time do you get up in the morning and go to bed at night? Draw how each time looks on an analog clock. | Measure the length of each of your fingers in either in. or cm. Which is the longest? The shortest? |
| **Week 20** | Write the numbers 1 to 20 in a line. Color the even numbers blue and the odd numbers red. What is the pattern? | Make play money by writing $1, $5, $10, and $20 on index cards. Draw three at a time and add the total number of dollars. | Open a book to two pages at random. Subtract the smaller page number from the larger one. Draw a number line to show your work. | Find a five-sided object in your home. What shape has five sides? |

| | Day 1 | Day 2 | Day 3 | Day 4 |
|---|---|---|---|---|
| Week 21 | Draw a number line from 1 to 12. Then, compare it to a ruler that has 12 in.. How are they the same? How are they different? | Ask a friend or family member to measure your height to the nearest foot. Then do the same for them. Who is taller? | Ask four of your friends or family members how many glasses of water they drink during the day. Make a bar graph to show the data. | Make flash cards for times of the day. Flip one card at a time and say where the hands would be on an analog clock. |

| | Day 1 | Day 2 | Day 3 | Day 4 |
|---|---|---|---|---|
| Week 22 | Get 100 pennies (or small items). Put them into groups to model quarters, dimes, and nickels. How many of each coin is 100¢? | Number index cards from 1 to 9. Pick three at a time to make three-digit numbers. Compare the numbers using <, >, and =. | Write a math word problem having to do with frogs. Have an adult or a friend solve it. | Look at a baking sheet. What kinds of arrays are made with food on a baking sheet? Write an addition number sentence for one. |

| | Day 1 | Day 2 | Day 3 | Day 4 |
|---|---|---|---|---|
| Week 23 | Measure the length of your pencil in in. and cm. Which measurement number is greater? Explain. | Have an adult cut three pieces of string. Measure them. Find the difference between lengths and the total length. | Find an object in your home that is a prism, but not a cube. Is the prism rectangular, triangular, or another shape? | Draw a number line with your age and the age of a family member. How much older or younger is your family member? |

| | Day 1 | Day 2 | Day 3 | Day 4 |
|---|---|---|---|---|
| Week 24 | Find or make a hundreds chart. Count by 5s, coloring in the numbers you say. What patterns do you see counting by 5s to 100? | Find a six-sided object in your home. What shape has six sides? | Number index cards from 1 to 9. Pick three at a time to make three-digit numbers. Practice subtracting the three-digit numbers. | Measure the length of a room with your feet. Then use a foot-long ruler. Which "foot" is longer, the ruler or your foot? |

| | Day 1 | Day 2 | Day 3 | Day 4 |
|---|---|---|---|---|
| Week 25 | Count the number of blue, red, yellow, and green crayons or other coloring tools you have. Make a bar graph to show the data. | Have an adult set an analog clock to different times. Tell the time to the nearest five minutes. | Make a list of things in your home you would measure in yards and a list of the things you would measure in in.. | Draw two rectangles that are the same size. Draw lines to divide the rectangles into different numbers of squares. |
| Week 26 | Divide a circle into fourths. Think: if everyone in my family got a fourth, would I need more? Would there be any left over? | Count the number of pillows in your room or your home. Is it even or odd? How many are squares? Circles? Rectangles? | Measure your foot and your shoe to the nearest centimeter. How much longer is your shoe than your foot? | List some things you would measure in feet and some you would measure in yards. Are there any you would use both for? |
| Week 27 | Make a set of cards that show the time in words and in numbers. Play a matching game with the cards. | Find or make a hundreds chart. Close your eyes and point to a number. Repeat three times, and add the four numbers together. | Number index cards from 1 to 9. Pick three at a time to make three-digit numbers. Say or write the numbers in expanded form. | Look at the foods in a single meal. Do you see any geometric shapes, or foods that are close to being geometric shapes? |
| Week 28 | Think of a shape. Have someone try to guess the shape, using only yes or no questions about its number of sides, faces, etc. | Measure a long, thin food like a carrot. Take a bite and measure again. Subtract to find the length of your bite. | Roll a pair of dice. Write a fact family for the two numbers that you roll. | Measure your height to the nearest inch, foot, and yard. Which measurement is the closest to your real height? Why? |

| | Day 1 | Day 2 | Day 3 | Day 4 |
|---|---|---|---|---|
| **Week 29** | Number index cards from 1 to 9. Pick three at a time to make a three-digit number. Then, rearrange the digits to change their place values. | Estimate the length of your hair in in.. Then have an adult measure it to the nearest inch to check your estimate. | Roll a sheet of paper into a tube. What 3-D shape did you make? Try to make other 3-D shapes with a sheet of paper. | Practice counting time. Starting with an hour (e.g. 7:00), count by groups of five minutes to the next hour. |

| | Day 1 | Day 2 | Day 3 | Day 4 |
|---|---|---|---|---|
| **Week 30** | Teach an adult how to add 501 + 103. | Write what time it is to the nearest five minutes. Use both an analog clock and a digital clock to tell the time. | Grab an even number of small snacks. Divide them in half and write a number sentence that describes your snacks. For example: 5 + 5 = 10. | Have someone in your family tell you three numbers from 0 to 9. What is the biggest three digit number you can make? |

| | Day 1 | Day 2 | Day 3 | Day 4 |
|---|---|---|---|---|
| **Week 31** | Skip count by 5s from 100 to 200. | Grab some raisins or another small snack and make an array. How many do you have? | Estimate the length of something in your room using cm. Then, measure to see if you are correct. | What is something in your home that you might count in a bundle of 100s? |

| | Day 1 | Day 2 | Day 3 | Day 4 |
|---|---|---|---|---|
| **Week 32** | Explain to an adult what a hundreds block is. What does it mean? | Find examples of triangles, quadrilaterals, pentagons, hexagons, and cubes around your home or outside. | What are two related subtraction facts for the fact family 15 + 4 = 19? | How can you tell whether a group of objects is even or odd? |

|  | **Day 1** | **Day 2** | **Day 3** | **Day 4** |
|---|---|---|---|---|
| **Week 33** | Draw a cake. Cut it into thirds. Draw a pie. Cut it into fourths. Draw a brownie. Cut it into halves. | Find three green things in your home. Estimate their lengths in in.. Then, measure to see if you are correct. | Ask your family members what their favorite room of the home is. Make a bar graph. | Measure six pencils to the nearest centimeter. Use the data to make a line plot. |

|  | **Day 1** | **Day 2** | **Day 3** | **Day 4** |
|---|---|---|---|---|
| **Week 34** | Borrow some change from an adult. How many cents do you have? | What time do you eat dinner? Record the time in words and numbers. | How many chairs are in your home? Is it an even number? Write an addition sentence to show how you know. | Have a family member tell you four digits from 0 to 9. Use the digits to make two 2-digit numbers. Use < and > to compare the numbers. |

|  | **Day 1** | **Day 2** | **Day 3** | **Day 4** |
|---|---|---|---|---|
| **Week 35** | Which is longer, a 2-inch ribbon or a 2-centimeter ribbon? Explain. | How many doors do you have in your home? How many windows? How many doors and windows altogether? | Play store with a friend or family member. When it is time to pay, give the cashier the exact sum needed without any extra. | You can use money to represent place value. Draw dollars, dimes and pennies. Can you show 503? 892? |

|  | **Day 1** | **Day 2** | **Day 3** | **Day 4** |
|---|---|---|---|---|
| **Week 36** | Measure seven short plants or other objects near your home to the nearest inch. Make a line plot with the data. | Measure one item in your kitchen in in. and in cm. How are the numbers different? Why? | Pick a small sum of money. What are two coin combinations you could use to make it? | Draw triangles, quadrilaterals, pentagons, hexagons, and cubes on index cards. Play a matching game. |

| | Day 1 | Day 2 | Day 3 | Day 4 |
|---|---|---|---|---|
| **Week 37** | What would be an appropriate tool to use to measure the length of a table? A beetle? A boat? | Find at least two arrays in your home. Write addition sentences for them. | Measure the height and width of a window in your room. Which is longer? By how much? | Write an addition word problem based on things in your home. |

| | Day 1 | Day 2 | Day 3 | Day 4 |
|---|---|---|---|---|
| **Week 38** | Estimate the height of each person in your family in cm. | Show an adult how to use a number line for addition. | Use a calculator and pre-written 3-digit addition problems to race against a family member to find the answers to the problems. | Draw a tabletop, and then partition it evenly so that six people could sit there. |

| | Day 1 | Day 2 | Day 3 | Day 4 |
|---|---|---|---|---|
| **Week 39** | Use small objects to show how an array is like an addition problem. | Explain decomposing with subtraction to an adult using dimes and pennies. | Go on a cube hunt. Count the number of items in your home that resemble a cube. Record the number. | Draw a robot. Place a 2-digit number in each arm and each leg. Then, add the numbers together to find the sum. |

| | Day 1 | Day 2 | Day 3 | Day 4 |
|---|---|---|---|---|
| **Week 40** | Explain to an adult how to mentally add a number, such as 500, to another number. | Draw a secret hideout. Use at least two quadrilaterals and one triangle. | Write a measurement word problem. Give it to an adult to solve. Check to see if she has the correct answer. | Find at least one shape with five angles. Tell an adult how the angles relate to the number of sides. |

Maddie has 3 bracelets, Rachael has 5 bracelets, and Hailey has 7 bracelets. How many bracelets are there?

_____ + _____ + _____ = _____

Divide into fourths.

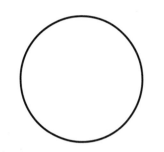

9 + 7 = _____

○ even

○ odd

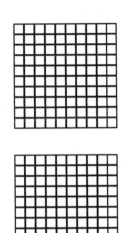

_____ hundreds

_____ tens

_____ ones

Draw a picture of a house. Use at least one of each shape: square, rectangle, triangle, trapezoid.

Show 8:30.

53 – 10 = _____

8 pennies

_____ ¢

Write **<**, **>**, or **=** to compare.

45 ○ 54          98 ○ 99

76 ○ 77          41 ○ 31

52 ○ 51          87 ○ 88

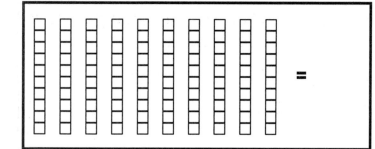  =

____ + ____ + ____ + ____ = ____

Philip has 38 crayons. He gets another box of 24 crayons. How many crayons does he have?

5 + 7 = ____

____ + 5 = 12

12 - ____ = 7

____ - 7 = 5

68
- 44
‾‾‾‾

Write the number.

1 ten and 6 ones

Write the number in words.

**143**

_____

_____

**888 - 100 = ____**

| Favorite After School Snacks | |
|---|---|
| Snack | Number of Students |
| Mini pretzels | 4 |
| Apple slices | 7 |
| Carrot sticks | 5 |

How many students like carrot sticks?
_____

How many more students like apple slices than mini pretzels? _____

How many students voted for their favorite snack? _____

Which number sentence is true?

○ 5 = 4 + 2     ○ 3 + 2 = 4 + 1

○ 4 = 6 - 3     ○ 5 - 3 = 4 - 1

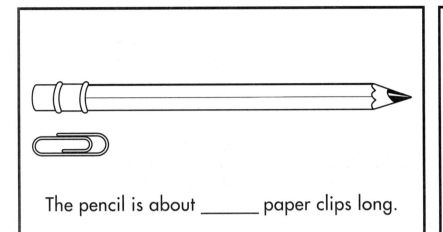

The pencil is about _____ paper clips long.

Partition the rectangle into 6 equal parts.

Yvette made 64 water balloons. Ross made 28. So far, they have popped 76 water balloons. How many water balloons are left?

○ Subtract. Then, add.

○ Subtract. Then, subtract again.

○ Add. Then, subtract.

○ Add. Then, add again.

5, 10, 15, _____, _____, _____

What am I?

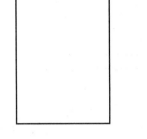

_____

What would be the best tool for measuring the length of your shoe?

○ ruler

○ yardstick

○ meterstick

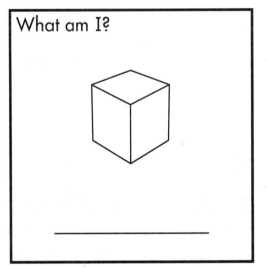

_____ ¢

eleven forty-five

Write the number.

4 tens and 2 ones

```
  42        63        27
+ 51      + 16      + 32
```

There are 34 people eating at the food court in the mall. Some more people arrive. Now there are 86 people. How many people came into the food court?

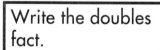

9 + ☆ = 17

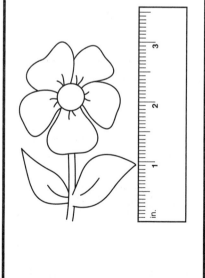

_____ apples

Cross out the base ten blocks to solve the problem.

**375 − 262 = _____**

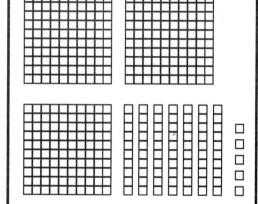

**70 − 10 =**

Draw a pentagon.

The flower is _____

inches tall.

Write the doubles fact.

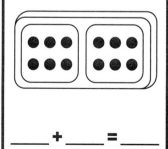

____ + ____ =

Write each number in expanded form.

**853 =** _____

**850 =** _____

Carlos had 45 pieces of popcorn. He ate some. Now he has 13 pieces of popcorn. How many pieces of popcorn did Carlos eat?

How much is shaded? _____

**443 – 100 =**

Circle the longest line segment.

Write the numbers and circle the operations to get from 23 to 47.

**23**

+ □
−

**34**

+ □
−

**19**

+ □
−

**47**

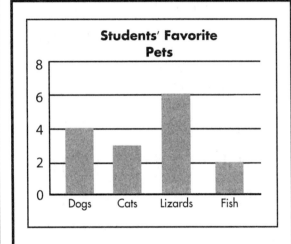

**Students' Favorite Pets**

How many more students like lizards than like fish? _____

How many students like cats or dogs? _____

**511**

_____ hundreds

_____ ten

_____ one

**15 – 9 + 5 =**

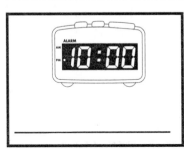

_____

Draw and label two ways to make 67¢.

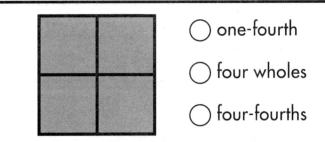

○ one-fourth

○ four wholes

○ four-fourths

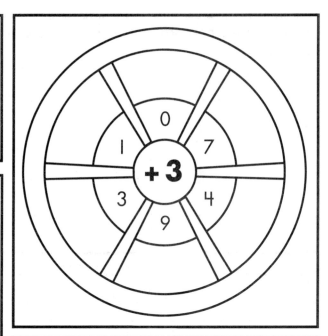

Write an addition number sentence to match the array.

Write **<**, **>**, or **=** to compare.

45 ○ 54

145 ○ 144

540 ○ 540

450 ○ 440

$$368 \\ + 132$$

$$24 \\ 36 \\ + 27$$

Color the box that has an odd number of dots.

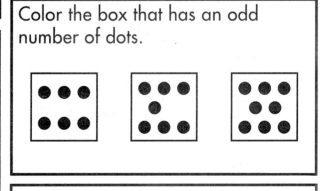

Measure to the nearest inch and centimeter.

_____ in.

_____ cm

283, 293, _____, _____, _____

Veronica has 34 cans and 39 bottles to recycle. How many items does she have altogether?

Match the problems whose answers are the same.

| | |
|---|---|
| 7 + 3 | 2 + 3 |
| 9 – 5 | 9 – 2 |
| 5 + 2 | 6 + 4 |
| 6 – 1 | 7 – 3 |

26 + 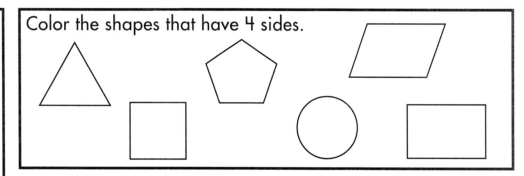 = 54

Which number sentence could you use to solve the problem?

○ 26 + 54 =

○ 54 – 26 =

○ 26 – 54 =

| | Students' Favorite Desserts |
|---|---|
| Cake | l l l l |
| Ice Cream | lllll l l l |
| Lollipop | l l l |

How many students like cake? ____

How many students like ice cream? ____

How many more students like ice cream than lollipops? ____

20 – 10 + 3 =

Draw an array to match the number sentence.

3 + 3 + 3 = 9

24
64
36
+ 46

Color the shapes that have 4 sides.

**509**

| Hundreds | Tens | Ones |
|---|---|---|
| | | |

Write the number.

6 hundreds

|  |  |  |
|---|---|---|
| 83 | 64 | 92 |
| − 51 | − 35 | − 27 |

What is the value of the underlined number?

**3<u>4</u>5**

○ four ones

○ four tens

○ four hundreds

Circle the greater number.

600 + 60 + 3

600 + 50 + 9

| Student | Number of Cousins |
|---|---|
| Ted | I I I |
| Marie | ⊬⊬⊬ I I I |
| Jonathan | ⊬⊬⊬ |

Who has the most cousins? _____

Who has the fewest cousins? _____

How many cousins do the students have in all? _____

Circle each pair of numbers that equals 12. Some pairs are side by side and others are up and down.

| 3 | 9 | 4 | 10 | 1 | 12 |
|---|---|---|---|---|---|
| 7 | 2 | 8 | 5 | 6 | 0 |
| 4 | 11 | 3 | 7 | 2 | 6 |
| 12 | 4 | 6 | 8 | 6 | 9 |
| 8 | 4 | 6 | 0 | 3 | 5 |
| 7 | 2 | 10 | 1 | 11 | 2 |

**989 − 100 =**

Write the number.

seven hundred thirty-two

Hilary has 17 books and 42 magazines on her bookshelf. Rebecca has 26 magazines on her bookshelf. How many more items are on Hilary's bookshelf?

Which is longer?

○ 1 inch

○ 1 centimeter

**76 − 31 =**

○ 35          ○ 45

○ 37          ○ 47

Ms. Pendleton had 75 gumballs in a jar. She gave 23 to her students. How many are left?

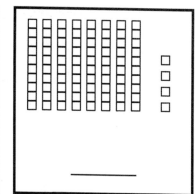

_____

**15 – 7 =**

Color an odd number of fish.

Color 349.

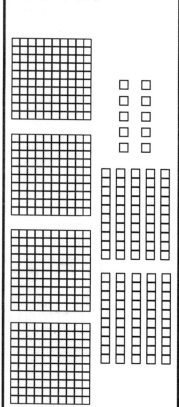

Draw 4 different triangles by adding to the lines provided.

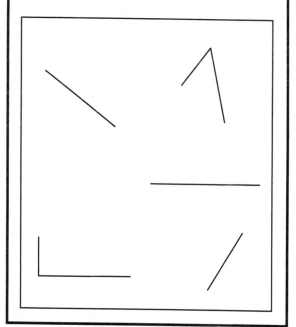

Show 1:30.

**20 + 10 =**

2 dimes, 3 nickels, 8 pennies

_____ ¢

_____ cm

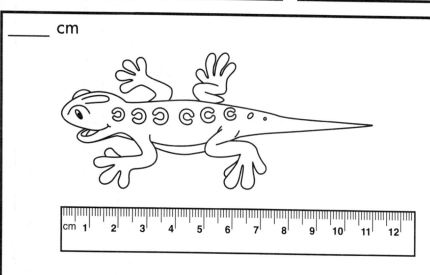

How many square units make up the rectangle? _____

Roberto has 33 blue building blocks, 30 red building blocks, and 27 yellow building blocks. How many blocks does he have?

Complete the fact family.

____ + 6 = 11

6 + 5 = ____

11 – ____ = 5

____ – 5 = 6

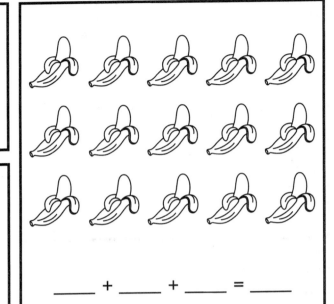

____ + ____ + ____ = ____

81
– 39

4 tens =

10 tens =

8 tens =

Write the number in words.

56

_____

497, 498, _____, _____, _____

4 + 5 – 7 + 9 =

12 – 5 + 7 – 3 =

**T-Shirt Colors**

8
7
6
5
4
3
2
1
0

Pink    Yellow    Green    Purple

How many students are wearing pink or yellow? _____
How many more students are wearing green than purple? _____
How many students are wearing T-shirts? _____

The brush is _____ centimeters longer than the comb.

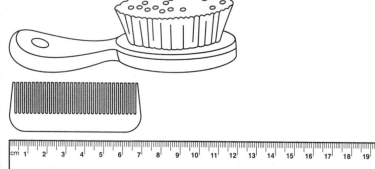

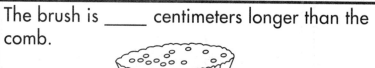

Draw a rectangle that is made up of 8 square units.

. . . . .

. . . . .

. . . . .

. . . . .

Katrina's hens laid 45 eggs. She sold 36 eggs. Then, the hens laid some more eggs. Now Katrina has 52 eggs. How many eggs did the hens lay the second time?

○ Subtract. Then, add.

○ Subtract. Then, subtract again.

○ Add. Then, subtract.

○ Add. Then, add again.

**70 – 50 =**

Draw a hexagon.

Estimate the length of your thumb in inches.

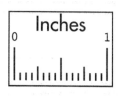

Inches

_____ inches

Circle the answer on the number line.

**3 + 4 = _____**

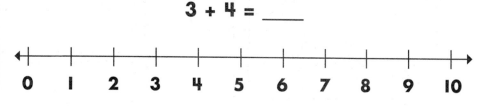

0  1  2  3  4  5  6  7  8  9  10

Ian had 25 marbles. He got 14 more. How many marbles does he have now?

Write **<**, **>**, or **=** to compare.

**764 ◯ 674**

```
  44        256       1 2 3
+ □1      + 2□2     + □□6
  75        498       3 5 9
```

Kurt has 88 songs on his music player. He has 23 more songs than Frederick. How many songs does Frederick have?

○ triangle
○ cone
○ sphere

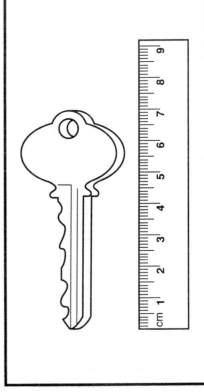 = _____ animals

Cross out the base ten blocks to subtract.

**489 – 148 = _____**

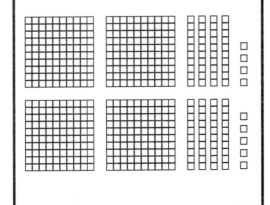

71 + _____ = 81

Write the number.

seven hundred eighty-nine

_____ cm

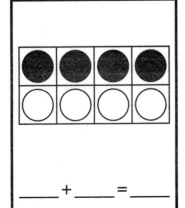

Write each number in expanded form.

67 = _____

670 = _____

_____ + _____ = _____

The bakery made 48 bagels and 36 doughnuts. After breakfast, there were only 23 items left. How many items sold during breakfast?

Draw base ten blocks to show **38**.

18 − 9 =

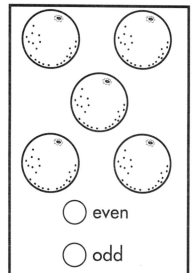

◯ even

◯ odd

Write the missing numbers.

13 − 7 = ⑥

◯ − 9 = ⑥

◯ − ◯ = 7

17 − ◯ = ◯

◯ − 5 = ◯

◯ − 6 = 8

Number of Flowers Picked

| Harvey | 🌸 🌸 🌸 🌸 |
| Melissa | 🌸 🌸 🌸 🌸 |
| Dan | 🌸 🌸 🌸 🌸 🌸 |
| Josie | 🌸 🌸 |

🌸 = 1 flower

Who picked the most flowers? _____

Who picked the fewest flowers? _____

Which students picked the same number of flowers? _____

**902**

_____ hundreds

_____ tens

_____ ones

5 + 6 + 5 =

five fifteen

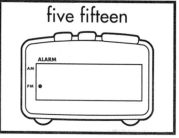

Write **<**, **>**, or **=** to compare.

25 ◯ 225          403 ◯ 303

54 ◯ 45          275 ◯ 285

137 ◯ 136          800 ◯ 80

Divide the squares into fourths two different ways.

Use addition to fill in the pyramid. Each number is the sum of the two numbers below it.

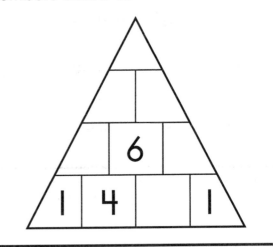

Draw an array for the number sentence.

1 + 1 + 1 + 1 + 1 = 5

Which one is part of the same fact family as the number sentence?

4 + 5 = 9

○ 5 + 9 = 4

○ 4 − 9 = 5

○ 9 − 5 = 4

○ 4 + 9 = 5

119
+ 183

37
23
46
+ 14

Write the missing numbers.

| 42 |    | 44 |
|----|----|----|
| 52 |    |    |
|    | 63 |    |

_____ in.

402, 401, _____, _____, _____

Ricky painted 13 feet of fence and Andrea painted 12 feet. How many feet of fence did they paint in all?

Match each item to the unit you would use to measure it.

height of a person      inches

length of a pencil      yards

length of a field      feet

---

☆ − 38 = 51

Which number sentence could you use to solve the problem?

○ 51 − 38 = ☆

○ 38 + 51 = ☆

○ 38 + 38 = ☆

---

Number of Books Students Read

```
          x
          x       x
  x       x       x       x
  x       x       x       x
-----------------------------
  2       3       4       5
```

How many students read four books? _____

What was the greatest number of books a student read? _____

How many students read books? _____

---

**70 =**

_____ tens + _____ ones

---

○ prism

○ circle

○ sphere

---

$$\begin{array}{r} 1\,9\,7 \\ -\ \boxed{\phantom{0}}\,4 \\ \hline 1\,4\,3 \end{array}$$

---

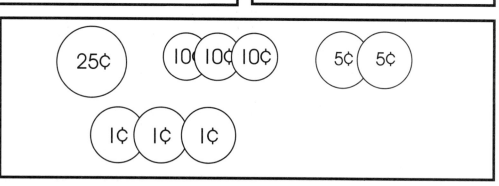

---

○ midnight

○ noon

---

512, 522,

_____, _____,

_____

459        264        768
- 236      -  51      - 503

Write the value of the 4 in each number.

364 ____              145 ____

450 ____              904 ____

Write <, >, or = to compare.

501 ◯ 510

| Students Who Can Whistle | |
| --- | --- |
| Mr. Bing's Class | ⊮⊮⊮ ‖ |
| Ms. Ellis's Class | ‖‖‖ |
| Ms. Nguyen's Class | ⊮⊮⊮ ⊮⊮⊮ ‖ |

Which teacher has the fewest students who can whistle? _____

How many more students in Ms. Nguyen's class can whistle than in Mr. Bing's class? ____

The numbers in the squares are the sums of the numbers in the circles. Write the missing numbers.

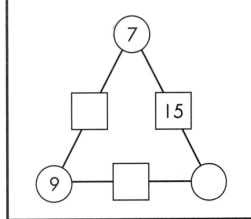

7 + 6 - 9 =

Write the number.

one hundred fifteen

Maurice had 78 sheets of notebook paper. He gave 24 sheets to Kevin and 24 sheets to Enrique. How many sheets of notebook paper does he have left?

Which has the greatest value?

◯ dime

◯ dollar

◯ quarter

173 - 41 =

◯ 32        ◯ 132

◯ 34        ◯ 134

Ruby has 72 plastic forks and 48 plastic spoons for a party. How many more forks than spoons does she have?

Color one-third of the circle.

**7 – 3 + 10 =**

What would you use to measure a computer screen?

◯ meterstick

◯ yardstick

◯ ruler

Color 178.

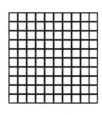

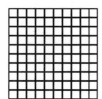

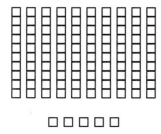

List the shapes you see in the truck.

_____ : _____

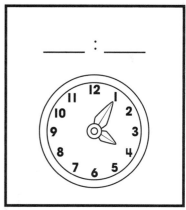

**801 – 100 =**

4 dimes, 1 nickel, 13 pennies

_____ ¢

_____ cm

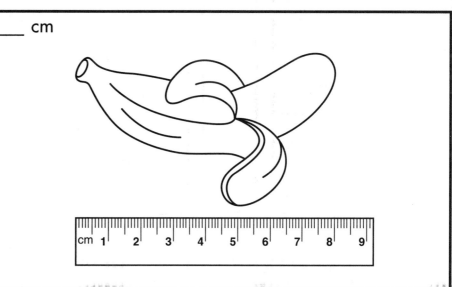

**33**

○ cylinder

○ circle

○ cone

Miranda had 47¢. She found a quarter and a nickel in the car seat. How much money does she have now?

Write **<**, **>**, or **=** to compare.

651 ○ 650

345 ○ 245

301 ○ 311

989 ○ 889

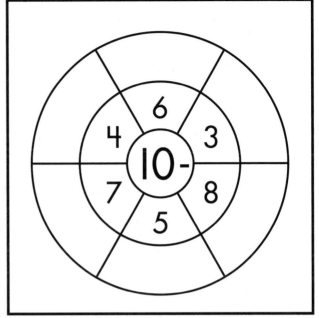

|   189  |
| −   75 |

Write the number.

three tens and six ones

Color the plant that has an odd number of leaves.

751, _____, 749, _____, _____

Trees at the Park

| Pine | ⊦⊦⊦⊦ | |
| Oak | | | | |
| Maple | ⊦⊦⊦⊦ |
| Ginkgo | | | |

How many trees are at the park? ____

How many more pine trees than ginkgo trees are there? ____

How many oaks are there? ____

Which number sentence is true?

○ 5 − 1 = 3      ○ 6 − 4 = 1

○ 3 + 2 = 6      ○ 4 + 1 = 5

How much longer is one adhesive bandage than the other? _____ cm

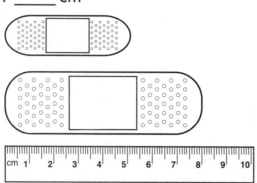

Divide the rectangles in half two different ways.

**Visits to Lucy's Grandparents' House**

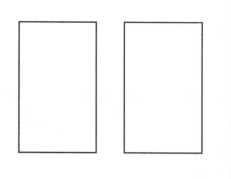

How many times did Lucy visit her grandparents?

_____

During which season did Lucy visit her grandparents the most? _____

**99 =**
_____ tens + _____ ones

Draw a rectangle that can be divided into 9 square units.

14
24
16
+ 26

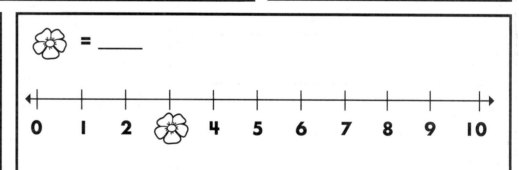

Kendra collected 23 blue stamps and 37 red stamps. How many stamps does she have?

30 + 50 =

Draw a picture or base ten blocks to explain how to solve the problem.

**28 – 19 =**

Joellyn did 35 sit-ups on Tuesday and 55 sit-ups on Friday. How many sit-ups did she do this week?

Circle the lesser number.

eight hundred nine

eight hundred ninety

Color an even number of lollipops.

Solve the addition problems to complete the puzzle.

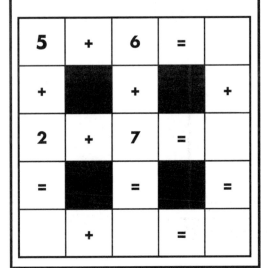

| 5 | + | 6 | = | |
|---|---|---|---|---|
| + | | + | | + |
| 2 | + | 7 | = | |
| = | | = | | = |
| | + | | = | |

**8 + 8 =**

Draw a half circle.

Yuri picked 79 blueberries. He ate a handful, and then picked 34 more. Now he has 96 blueberries. How many did he eat?

Write the doubles facts.

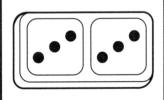

___ + ___ = ___

Write each number in expanded form.

**399** = _____

**234** = _____

Name _____

Felicity has 57 feet of fishing line. Matt has 36 feet of fishing line. How many feet of fishing line do they have altogether?

_____

14 − 8 =

What would you use to measure the height of a building?

◯ inches

◯ meters

◯ centimeters

Skip count by 10s down the ladder.

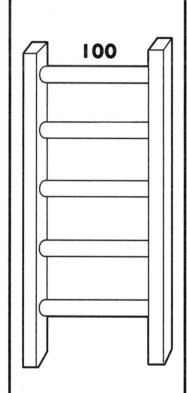

100

| Renee's Garden | |
|---|---|
| Tomato plants | ⊦⊦⊦⊦ l |
| Cucumber plants | l l l l |
| Squash plants | ⊦⊦⊦⊦ |

Which plant does Renee have the most of? _____

How many plants does Renee have in her garden? _____

How many more tomato than squash plants are there? _____

Write the number.

4 hundreds, 2 tens, 8 ones

15 − 5 + 7 =

four thirty

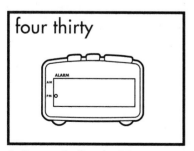

Draw and label two ways to make 25¢.

edges _____

faces _____

vertices _____

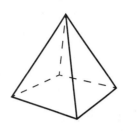

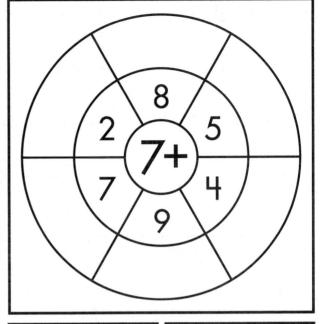

Draw an array to match the number sentence.

4 + 4 + 4 = 12

Write **<**, **>**, or **=** to compare.

34 ◯ 24

78 ◯ 87

56 ◯ 57

46 ◯ 46

676
+ 134

Write the number.

2 tens

Write the missing numbers.

| 122 |     |     |
|-----|-----|-----|
|     | 133 |     |
|     | 143 | 144 |

340 − 100 = _____

Measure to the nearest inch and centimeter.

_____ in.

_____ cm

The florist had 50 roses. Mario bought 18 roses. How many roses are left?

Match the shape to correct description.

**triangle**          **4 sides, 4 angles**

**quadrilateral**     **no sides, no angles**

**circle**            **3 sides, 3 angles**

---

Which number sentence is true?

○ 6 – 3 = 3

○ 2 + 4 = 5

○ 4 – 2 = 1

---

There were 45 people at the grocery store and 30 people at the library. Then, 16 people left the grocery store and went to the library. How many people are at each place now?

○ Add. Then, add again.

○ Subtract. Then, subtract again.

○ Add. Then, subtract.

---

**6 – 5 + 7 + 7 =**

Write a number sentence to match the array.

---

Which estimate for the length of a banana is best?

○ 7 inches

○ 7 feet

○ 7 yards

---

Write the missing numbers.

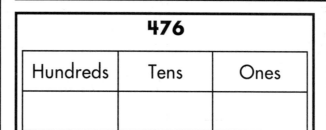

0   10        30   40        60   70        90   100

---

| 476 | | |
|---|---|---|
| Hundreds | Tens | Ones |
|  |  |  |

---

Write **<**, **>**, or **=** to compare.

**78** ○ **67**

```
   3 7          4 1          2 5
 + 5 □        + □ 8        + □ 1
 ───────      ───────      ───────
   8 9          7 9          9 6
```

What is the value of the underlined digit?

**8<u>9</u>0**

○ 9

○ 90

○ 900

Circle the greater number.

100 + 9

100 + 20

Color the even numbers to reveal the hidden picture.

| 15 | 7  | 11 | 17 | 9  | 1  | 3  |
|----|----|----|----|----|----|----|
| 3  | 19 | 8  | 5  | 16 | 7  | 11 |
| 13 | 1  | 9  | 3  | 19 | 5  | 15 |
| 17 | 5  | 7  | 11 | 5  | 13 | 7  |
| 19 | 20 | 15 | 13 | 9  | 18 | 9  |
| 5  | 13 | 10 | 6  | 4  | 13 | 5  |
| 1  | 19 | 7  | 5  | 11 | 9  | 17 |

Cross out the base ten blocks to subtract.

**537 − 426 = _____**

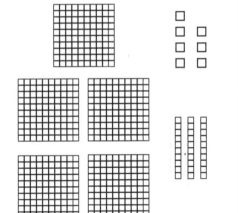

**40 + 50 =**

Write the number.

nine hundred ninety

_____ cm

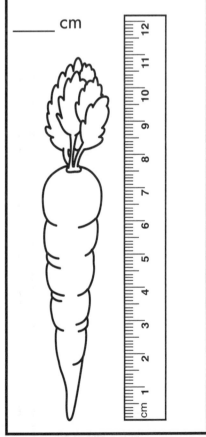

Which measurement is longer?

○ yard

○ foot

**77 − 44 =**

○ 31          ○ 33

○ 32          ○ 34

Ms. Farley has 56 art students. She has 43 paintbrushes. How many more does she need to get for each student to have a brush?

Color two-thirds.

$10 + 7 =$

Is the number of triangles even or odd? _____

$4 + 5 = \bigcirc$

$2 + \bigcirc = \bigcirc$

$4 + \bigcirc = \bigcirc$

$\bigcirc + 6 = \bigcirc$

$\bigcirc + \bigcirc = 8$

$9 + \bigcirc = 12$

Draw a robot using geometric shapes. List the shapes you use.

____ : ____

$9 - 3 + 8 =$

39 pennies and 1 nickel

_____ ¢

| Number Words | Hundreds ____ |
| two hundred fourteen | Tens ____ |
| | Ones ____ |
| Expanded Form | Base Ten Blocks |

Divide the rectangle into 7 equal parts.

Use addition to fill in the pyramid. Each number is the sum of the two numbers below it.

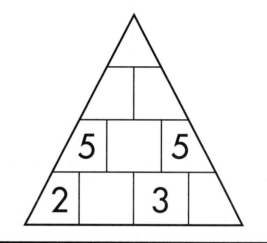

Malini made 72 samosas for her family reunion. Her family ate 54 samosas. How many samosas are left over?

Write the fact family for the numbers.

**3    4    7**

___ + ___ = ___

___ + ___ = ___

___ - ___ = ___

___ - ___ = ___

$$\begin{array}{r} 207 \\ -\ 56 \\ \hline \end{array}$$

$$\begin{array}{r} 35 \\ 72 \\ +\ 55 \\ \hline \end{array}$$

Color the box that has an odd number of tallies.

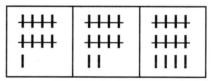

**Students' Favorite Drinks**

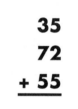

How many students like water best? _____

How many more students like soda than lemonade? _____

How many students like milk? _____

**300 + 100 =**

**18 – 9 + 7 – 8 =**

How much longer is one fork
than the other?

_____ cm

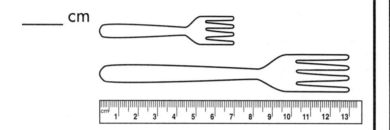

Ivan picked 88 strawberries.
He gave some to his
grandmother. Now he has
34 strawberries. How many
did he give away?

Mendez Family Favorite Sports

| Soccer | 卌 I I |
| Baseball | I I I I |
| Football | I I I |
| Volleyball | I I I I |

How many more family members like soccer than
football? _____

Which two sports do the same number of family
members like? _____

How many people are in the Mendez family?

_____

**61 =**
_____ **tens +** _____ **one**

Draw a rectangle that can
be divided into 10 equal
pieces.

. . . . . .

. . . . . .

. . . . . .

. . . . . .

. . . . . .

. . . . . .

Color the 3-dimensional shapes.

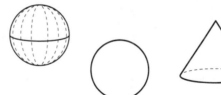

Robin had 40 trees behind her
house. Thirteen fell down in a
storm. How many trees does she
have now?

14 − 7 =

7 + 8 =

City Park Zoo has 65 species of land animals and 12 species of sea creatures. City Park Aquarium has 50 species of sea creatures. How many more species does the zoo have?

---

Write the value of the 2 in each number.

**425** ____        **632** ____

**203** ____        **812** ____

---

How many sides does a hexagon have?

○ **5**   ○ **6**   ○ **7**

---

The numbers in the squares are the sums of the numbers in the circles. Write the missing numbers.

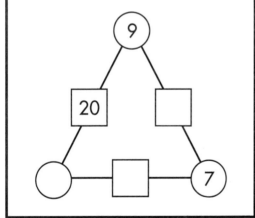

---

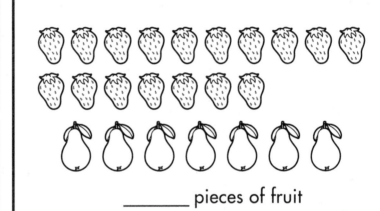

_____ pieces of fruit

---

**10 + 90 =**

---

Write the number word.

18

_____

---

Ms. Rivera's class has 20 students, Mr. Singh's class has 22 students, and Ms. O'Brian's class has 24 students. How many students do the teachers have altogether?

---

____ inch(es)

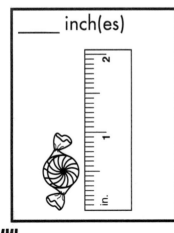

---

**500 + 40 + 2 = _____**

**90 + 7 = _____**

**100 + 80 = _____**

Gerald has 32 pairs of socks. Emmett has 19 pairs of socks. How many more pairs of socks does Gerald have?

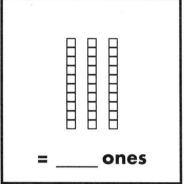

= _____ **ones**

15 + 4 =

Circle the shortest line segment.

_____

_____

_____

_____

Draw base ten blocks to match the number.

**234**

| Jelly Bean Colors | |
|---|---|
| Red | ‖‖‖ ‖‖‖ ‖‖‖ ‖ |
| Yellow | ‖‖‖ ‖‖‖ ‖ |
| Green | ‖‖‖ ‖‖‖ ‖‖‖ |

How many jelly beans are green? _____

How many more jelly beans are red than yellow? _____

How many jelly beans are there in all? _____

Write the number.

5 hundreds 9 tens 3 ones

80 – 20 =

six thirty

Draw and label two ways to make 35¢.

Color the sphere.

The library owns 99 DVDs. Now, 67 are checked out. How many DVDs are still available?

Write **<**, **>**, or **=** to compare each pair of numbers.

811 ◯ 801

456 ◯ 455

200 ◯ 190

730 ◯ 740

678
+ 219

54

_____ tens

_____ ones

Write the number in words.

**700 + 30 + 8**

_____

_____

252, _____, _____, 249, _____

Which number sentence is true?

◯ 5 = 3 + 3    ◯ 6 = 5 + 2

◯ 7 = 3 + 4    ◯ 4 = 3 + 2

_____ cm

Match the equal numbers.

455                     four hundred sixty-five

400 + 60 + 5      546

500 + 40 + 6      four hundred fifty-five

---

Draw a circle. Divide it in half.

---

Mandy needs 54 blue beads and 36 green beads for a bracelet. So far, she has collected a total of 67 beads. How many more beads does she need?

○ Subtract. Then, add.

○ Subtract. Then, subtract again.

○ Add. Then, subtract.

○ Add. Then, add again.

---

5 + 4 – 7 + 10 =

---

Write a number sentence to match the array.

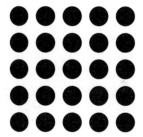

---

Estimate the length of a loaf of sandwich bread.

○ 1 foot

○ 1 yard

○ 1 meter

---

What does the number line show?

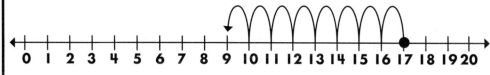

○ 17 – 9          ○ 9 + 8          ○ 17 – 8

---

Write the time words.

_____

---

Write the number.

4 hundreds

---

$$45 \atop + \, 36$$   $$76 \atop - \, 38$$   $$28 \atop + \, 59$$

Meredith knows 14 songs on the flute and 25 songs on the piano. How many songs does she know altogether?

Circle the larger number.

600 + 70 + 1

600 + 80

| Birds at the Bird Feeder | |
|---|---|
| Finch | I I I I |
| Sparrow | ⫫⫫ I I I |
| Cardinal | I I |

How many birds are at the bird feeder? _____

How many more sparrows than cardinals are there? _____

Solve the subtraction puzzle.

| 20 | – | 10 | = | |
|---|---|---|---|---|
| – | ■ | – | ■ | – |
| 5 | – | 3 | = | |
| = | ■ | = | ■ | = |
| | – | | = | |

6 + 3 =

Draw a quadrilateral.

_____ cm

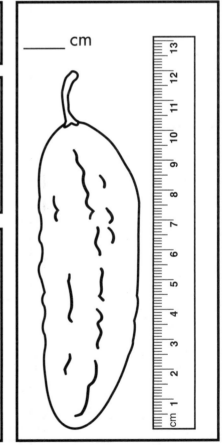

Draw an array to match the number sentence.

1 + 1 + 1 = 3

36 – 14 =

○ 20     ○ 22

○ 21     ○ 23

Frida made 48 cookies. She gave some away. Then she made 48 more cookies. Now she has 68 cookies. How many cookies did she give away?

Divide the square into 4 equal parts.

$5 + 3 - 4 =$

Color the box that has an odd number of dots.

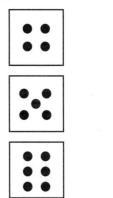

Circle the operations and write the numbers to get from 15 to 25.

**15**

$+$ ☐
$-$
_____

**38**

$+$ ☐
$-$
_____

**79**

$+$ ☐
$-$
_____

**25**

Hair Length in Inches

```
                              x
              x               x
x             x       x       x
x             x   x   x       x
```
_____

**1    2    3    4    5    6**

How many people have hair 3 inches long? _____

How many more people have 6-inch hair than 4-inch hair?

_____

How many people's hair was measured? _____

Show 10:00.

$169 - 100 =$

3 nickels and 7 pennies

_____ ¢

Write **<**, **>**, or **=** to compare.

567 ◯ 566       231 ◯ 221

802 ◯ 702       607 ◯ 617

311 ◯ 311       488 ◯ 480

How many faces does a cylinder have?

____ faces

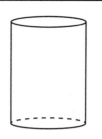

Tyler ate 35 peas. He still has 27 peas on his plate. How many peas did he start with?

Write the fact family for the numbers.

**8    9    17**

___ + ___ = ___

___ + ___ = ___

___ − ___ = ___

___ − ___ = ___

___ + ___ + ___ + ___

= ___

241
− 139

19
31
+ 25

Write the missing numbers.

| 347 |     |     |
|-----|-----|-----|
|     | 358 |     |
|     |     | 369 |

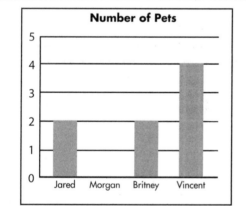

**Number of Pets**

Which student has no pets? _____

Which students have the same number of pets? _____

Which student has the most pets?

_____

899, 799, _____, _____, _____

Emily planted a tree that was 4 feet tall. Twenty years later, the tree was 38 feet tall. How much did it grow?

Measure to the nearest inch and centimeter.

____ in.

____ cm

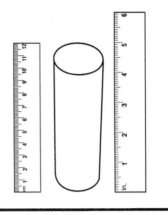

Draw and name a shape that has three sides.

_____

| Scoops of Ice Cream Eaten | |
|---|---|
| Danny | 🍨 🍨 |
| Jose | 🍨 🍨 🍨 |
| Hilary | 🍨 |

🍨 = 1 scoop

Who ate the least ice cream? _____

Who ate the most ice cream? _____

How much ice cream did the students eat altogether? _____

**89 =**
**____ tens + ____ ones**

Draw an array to match the number sentence.

**2 + 2 + 2 + 2 = 8**

$$\begin{array}{r} 15 \\ 34 \\ 45 \\ + 23 \\ \hline \end{array}$$

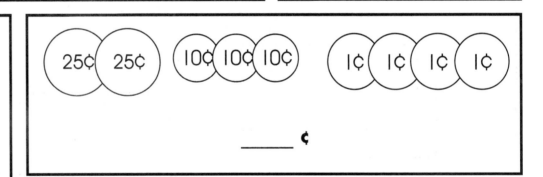

____ ¢

| 301 | | |
|---|---|---|
| Hundreds | Tens | Ones |
| | | |

Write <, >, or = to compare.

**25 ◯ 35**

```
  453        496        527
+ 275      - 342      + 128
```

What is the value of the 6 in each number?

426 ____          640 ____

162 ____          706 ____

Circle the greater number.

five hundred eighty

five hundred eighteen

Which number sentence matches the picture?

○ 2 + 3 = 5

○ 4 + 2 = 6

○ 4 + 3 = 7

Cross out the base ten blocks to subtract.

**335 − 311 = ____**

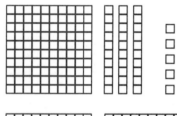

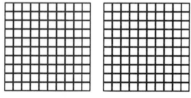

**392 + 10 =**

Write the number in words.

**27**

_____

The vending machine has 28 packs of gum and 46 snacks. How many items are in the vending machine?

Write the doubles fact.

____ + ____ = ____

**400 + 60 =**

**400 + 6 =**

**400 + 10 + 6 =**

Kurt had 87 chips. He gave 23 to Philip and 27 to Samson. How many chips does he have left?

_____

$14 + 4 =$

Which unit would be best for measuring a wall?

◯ in.

◯ cm

◯ meters

$9 + 7 = \bigcirc$

$\bigcirc + 8 = \bigcirc$

$\bigcirc + 3 = \bigcirc$

$\bigcirc + 9 = \bigcirc$

$\bigcirc + \bigcirc = 12$

$10 + \bigcirc = 20$

Draw a shape with four sides and four angles.

_____ hundred(s)

$8 + 6 - 7 =$

five minutes after eleven

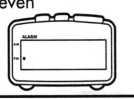

How much longer is one stick than the other?

_____ cm

Divide the rectangle into 6 equal parts.

Use addition to fill in the pyramid. Each number is the sum of the two numbers below it.

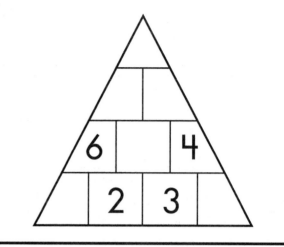

Tara had 46 rocks in her collection. She found 13 new rocks over the weekend. How many rocks does she have now?

Write **<**, **>**, or **=** to compares.

**750** ◯ **550**

**321** ◯ **320**

**873** ◯ **863**

**428** ◯ **389**

```
  347
+ 287
```

```
   23
   59
+ 41
```

Write the number in words.

**353**

_____

_____

**583 – 100 = ____**

**10 + 8 – 3 + 5 =**

____ cm

Match each shape to its name.

**square**

**cone**

**cube**

Rashad has 36 erasers. Felicia has 23 erasers. How many more erasers does Rashad have?

Eleanor's cookie recipe calls for 50 walnuts and 38 macadamia nuts. She has 48 nuts. How many more nuts does she need?

- ○ Subtract. Then, add.

- ○ Subtract. Then, subtract again.

- ○ Add. Then, subtract.

- ○ Add. Then, add again.

**5 + 6 + 8 =**

Draw a shape that has three angles.

$$
\begin{array}{r}
37 \\
82 \\
41 \\
+ \ 33 \\
\hline
\end{array}
$$

Draw on the number line to solve the problem.

**40 + 30 = ____**

0   10   20   30   40   50   60   70   80   90   100

Write the time in words.

_____

Write **<**, **>**, or **=** to compare.

**340 ○ 420**

145        299        656
+ 239      + 342      + 122

Write the value of the underlined digit.

1<u>9</u>0 ____        4<u>2</u>6 ____

53<u>2</u> ____        <u>3</u>77 ____

870, 860, _____, _____, _____

Color an even number of turtles.

The numbers in the squares are the sums of the numbers in the circles. Write the missing numbers.

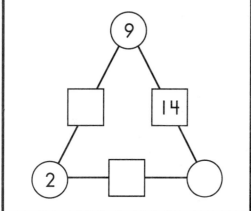

1 + 8 =

How many faces?

____

How much longer is one spoon than the other?

____ cm

____ cm

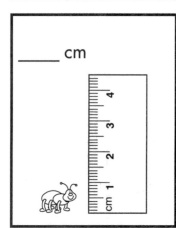

Write the numbers in expanded form.

**360** = _____

**433** = _____

The tire shop has 36 truck tires and 48 car tires. How many tires does it have in all?

Divide the square into 2 equal triangles.

$13 + 4 =$

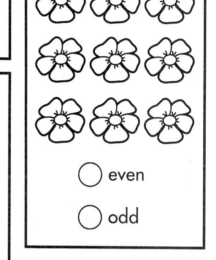

○ even

○ odd

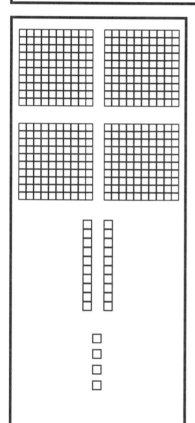

$533 + 100 =$

2 quarters and 3 dimes

_____ ¢

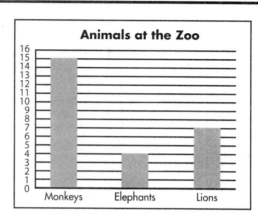

Which animal does the zoo have the most of? _____

Which animal does the zoo have the fewest of? _____

How many more monkeys than lions does the zoo have? _____

____ : ____

| Number Words | Hundreds ____ |
| --- | --- |
| | Tens ____ |
| | Ones ____ |
| Expanded Form<br>**300 + 8** | Base Ten Blocks |

_____ faces

_____ edges

_____ vertices

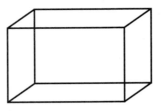

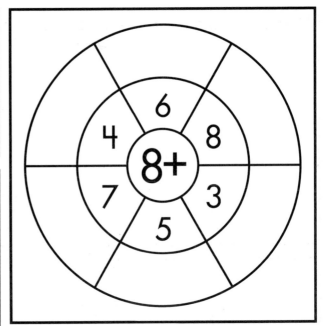

Draw an array to match the number sentence.

**2 + 2 + 2 + 2 + 2 + 2 + 2 = 14**

Write the fact family for the numbers.

**3      6      9**

___ + ___ = ___

___ + ___ = ___

___ − ___ = ___

___ − ___ = ___

56
+ 37

**441**

_____ hundreds

_____ tens

_____ one

Color the box that has an even number of tallies.

Caterpillar Lengths (cm)

```
x
x
x        x
x        x              x
x        x              x    x
_____
1        2        3        4        5
```

How long was the longest caterpillar?

_____

Which length had the most caterpillars?

_____

How many caterpillars are 3 centimeters long? _____

675, 680, _____, _____, _____

There are 77 grape sodas and 54 orange sodas. How many more sodas are grape?

Measure to the nearest inch and centimeter.

_____ in.

_____ cm

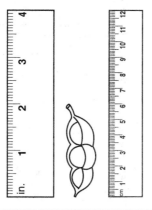

---

Which number sentence could you use to solve the problem?

**34 + ? = 88**

○ 34 – 88 = ?

○ 88 + 34 = ?

○ 88 – 34 = ?

---

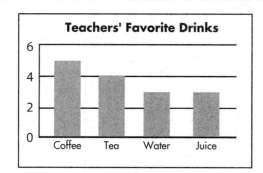

How many more teachers like coffee than tea?

_____

Which drinks do the same number of teachers like? _____

How many teachers were surveyed? _____

---

**4 + 10 – 9 =**

---

Draw a rectangle that can be divided into 12 equal parts.

. . . . . . .

. . . . . . .

. . . . . . .

. . . . . . .

. . . . . . .

. . . . . . .

---

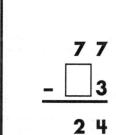

```
  7 7
- □ 3
─────
  2 4
```

---

25¢    5¢

1¢  1¢  1¢  1¢  1¢  1¢        _____ ¢

---

**727**

| Hundreds | Tens | Ones |
| --- | --- | --- |
|  |  |  |

---

Write **<**, **>**, or **=** to compare.

**350** ○ **340**

Ravi had 67 blocks. He gave some to Tanisha. Then, he got 23 more blocks. Now he has 56 blocks. How many blocks did he give away?

Write the value of the 3 in each number.

324 ____          370 ____

535 ____          893 ____

Circle the lesser number.

four hundred forty

four hundred fifty

Write a number sentence to macth the picture.

| 6 | + | 5 | = | |
|---|---|---|---|---|
| + | ■ | + | ■ | + |
| 3 | + | 4 | = | |
| = | ■ | = | ■ | = |
| | + | | = | |

322 – 10 =

Write the number in words.
622

_____

_____

Marie has 15 T-shirts. Her dad has 17 T-shirts and her brother has 14 T-shirts. How many T-shirts does Marie's family have in all?

Draw an array to match the number sentence.

2 + 2 = 4

33
+ 58

63
– 39

Dennis planted 56 seeds. Only 41 plants grew. How many seeds did not grow?

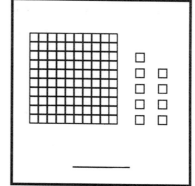

_____

15 – 11 =

Choose the best estimate.

◯ 1 inch

◯ 3 inches

◯ 5 inches

Count by 5s up the ladder

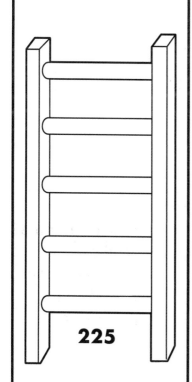

**225**

Label the shapes in the boat.

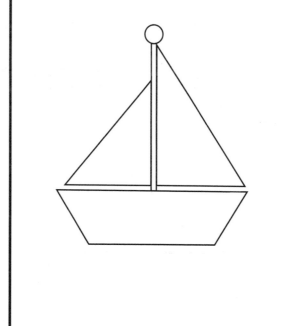

**664**

_____ hundreds

_____ tens

_____ ones

13 + 7 =

nine thirty-five

Measure the grapes to the nearest inch and centimeter.

_____ in.

_____ cm

◯ cone

◯ triangular prism

◯ pyramid

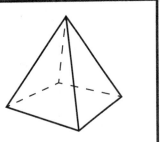

Write a number sentence to match the array.

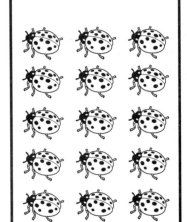

Write **<**, **>**, or **=** to compare.

**555** ◯ **554**

**242** ◯ **252**

**304** ◯ **294**

**112** ◯ **112**

```
  83
- 47
```

```
  24
  66
+ 53
```

Write the number in words.

**777**

_____

_____

120, 119, _____, _____, _____

Abby's pet snake is 33 in. long. Justin's snake is 18 in. long. How much longer is Abby's snake?

How much longer is one leaf than the other?

_____ cm

Match each shape to the number of faces.

| | |
|---|---|
| **cube** | 1 |
| **pyramid** | 2 |
| **cylinder** | 6 |
| **cone** | 5 |

Samantha has 90¢. She spends 60¢ on a candy bar. How many cents does she have left?

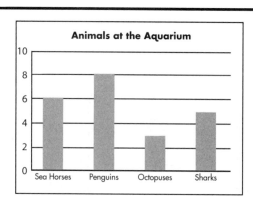

Which animal does the aquarium have the most of? _____

How many more sea horses than octopuses are there? _____

How many sharks does the aquarium have? ____

$4 + 15 - 7 =$

I have 4 sides and 4 angles. What am I?

○ triangle

○ trapezoid

○ half circle

34
72
14
+ 20

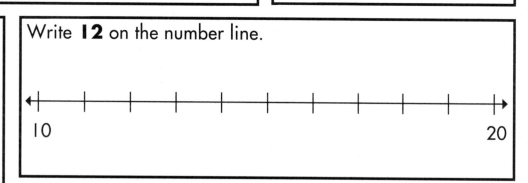
Write **12** on the number line.

10                                                  20

Write the time in words.

_____

$14 + 6 =$

$12 - 11 =$

```
  45          82          71
- 27        - 55        - 39
```

Reina needs 72 in. of fabric to make a tablecloth. She has 59 in. of fabric. How many more in. does she need?

Circle the greater number.

500 + 80 + 4

500 + 90

Which number sentence matches the picture?

○ 6 – 4 = 2

○ 6 + 4 = 10

○ 10 – 6 = 4

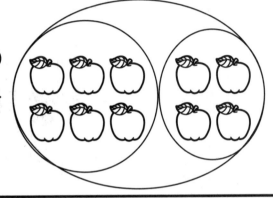

The numbers in the squares are the sums of the numbers in the circles. Write the missing numbers.

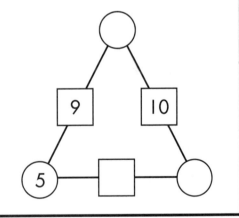

16 – 12 =

Write the number.

three hundred twenty-nine

_____ cm

Choose the best estimate for the length of an apple.

○ 4 feet

○ 4 inches

○ 4 yards

300 + 90 + 8 =

500 + 60 + 3 =

400 + 20 + 2 =

Jade bought 65 cupcakes for a party. Her guests ate 39 cupcakes. Then, she gave 15 cupcakes to her neighbor. How many cupcakes are left?

How much of the circle is shaded?

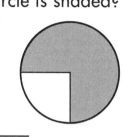

_____

200 + 10 =

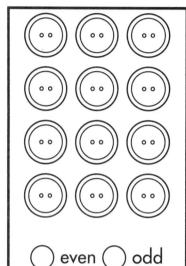

◯ even ◯ odd

Write the numbers and circle the operations to get from 22 to 48.

**22**

+ □
–

**59**

+ □
–

**16**

+ □
–

**48**

| Number of Cookies Sold at the Bake Sale | |
|---|---|
| Room A | 🍪 🍪 🍪 🍪 🍪 |
| Room B | 🍪 🍪 🍪 |
| Room C | 🍪 🍪 🍪 🍪 |

🍪 = 2 cookies

How many more cookies did Room A sell than Room B? _____

How many cookies did Room B sell? _____

How many cookies sold in all?
_____

_____ : _____

467 – 100 =

3 dimes and 46 pennies

_____ ¢

Write **<**, **>**, or **=** to compare.

354 ◯ 454          499 ◯ 509

276 ◯ 267          899 ◯ 901

511 ◯ 510          933 ◯ 934

_____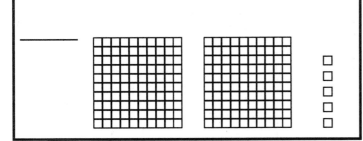

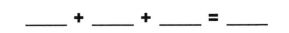
___ + ___ + ___ = ___

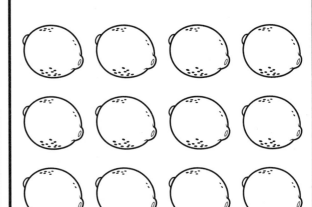

| Misty has 14 plates, 20 glasses, and 9 coffee mugs. How many items does she have? | Write the fact family for the numbers.  **2   7   9**  ___ + ___ = ___  ___ + ___ = ___  ___ − ___ = ___  ___ − ___ = ___ |
|---|---|

|  355  − 24  |  52  33  + 47  |
|---|---|

Write the missing numbers.

|     | 155 |     |
|-----|-----|-----|
|     |     | 166 |
| 174 |     |     |

How many in. longer is one straw than the other?

____ in.

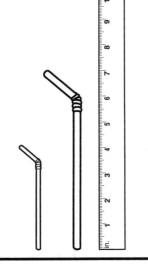

876, _____, 874, _____, _____

Which number sentence is true?

○ 3 + 2 = 4     ○ 4 − 3 = 1

○ 5 − 4 = 2     ○ 2 + 1 = 4

_____ in.

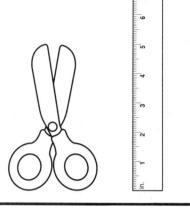

Divide the rectangle into thirds.

Marsha had 90 beads. She made a bracelet with 36 beads and then bought some more beads. Now she has 96 beads. How many beads did she buy?

- ◯ Subtract. Then, add.

- ◯ Subtract. Then, subtract again.

- ◯ Add. Then, subtract.

- ◯ Add. Then, add again.

$17 - 9 + 5 =$

Color the quadrilateral.

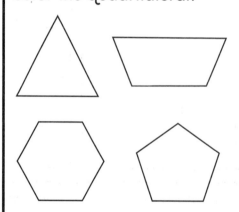

$$\begin{array}{r} 1\ \boxed{\phantom{0}}\ 6 \\ -\ \ 4\ 6 \\ \hline 1\ 3\ 0 \end{array}$$

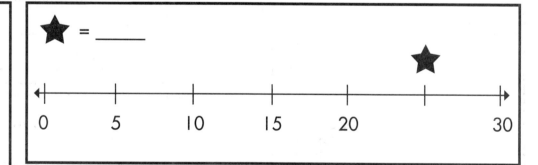

★ = _____

Danny has 24 moths and 35 butterflies in his insect collection. How many insects does he have?

Write **<**, **>**, or **=** to compare.

**359** ◯ **329**

Francesca picked 37 tomatoes and 19 peppers from her garden. She used 20 of the vegetables to make salsa. How many does she have left?

The library has 18 parking spaces in front of the building and 14 parking spaces behind. How many parking spaces in all?

How many sides does a pentagon have?

○ 4    ○ 5    ○ 6

Cross out the base ten blocks to subtract.

**476 – 345 = ____**

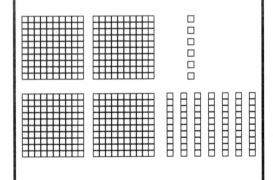

**= ____ ducks**

**442 + 10 =**

```
  390
- 189
```

____ in.

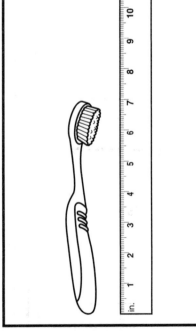

Write the doubles fact.

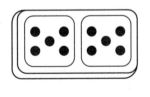

____ + ____ = ____

```
  540      239
- 277    + 239
```

Tina is 47 inches tall. Her little sister is 35 inches tall. How many inches taller is Tina?

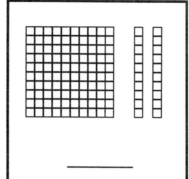

_____

20 – 17 =

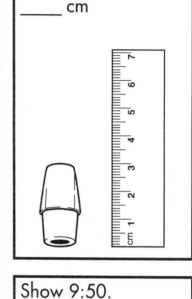

_____ cm

20 – 10 = ◯

15 – ◯ = ◯

13 – ◯ = ◯

17 – ◯ = ◯

◯ – ◯ = 7

◯ – 8 = 8

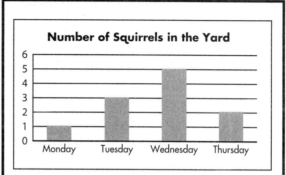

How many more squirrels were in the yard on Tuesday than Monday? _____

What day did the most squirrels come to the yard? _____

How many squirrels came to the yard on Thursday? _____

Show 9:50.

750 – 100 =

2 nickels and 1 quarter

_____ ¢

| Number Words | Hundreds _____ |
| --- | --- |
| | Tens _____ |
| | Ones _____ |
| Expanded Form | Base Ten Blocks |

Divide the rectangle into 5 equal parts.

Use addition to fill in the pyramid. Each number is the sum of the two numbers below it.

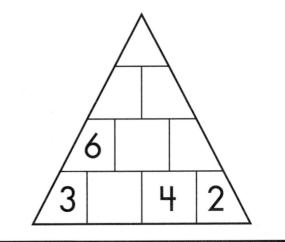

Freddie put 24 pepperoni on a medium pizza and 32 pepperoni on a large pizza. How many pepperoni did he use?

Write **<**, **>**, or **=** to compare.

340 ◯ 360

278 ◯ 280

542 ◯ 542

364 ◯ 370

$$\begin{array}{r} 454 \\ + 389 \\ \hline \end{array}$$

$$\begin{array}{r} 57 \\ 33 \\ + 45 \\ \hline \end{array}$$

Color the box that has an even number of dots.

Pencil Lengths in Inches

```
                x
    x           x
    x           x       x
    x       x   x       x
  _____
    4       5   6       7
```

How many pencils were 7 inches long?

_____

How many more pencils were 6 inches than 5 inches? _____

How many pencils were measured? _____

888 – 100 = _____

15 – 9 + 10 – 7 = _____

Measure to the nearest inch and centimeter.

_____ in.

_____ cm

How many thirds of the circle are shaded? _____

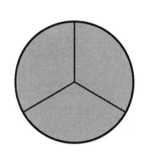

| Number of Houseplants | |
|---|---|
| Diana | 🌼 🌼 🌼 |
| Manuel | 🌼 🌼 🌼 🌼 🌼 🌼 🌼 🌼 |
| Isaac | 🌼 🌼 🌼 🌼 🌼 🌼 |

🌼 = 1

Who has the most houseplants? _____

Who has the fewest houseplants? _____

How many houseplants are there in all? _____

16 – 10 + 9 – 7 =

Draw an array to match the number sentence.

1 + 1 + 1 + 1 = 4

25
67
55
+ 39

Color the shapes that have 4 sides.

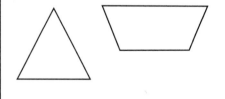

| 714 | | |
|---|---|---|
| Hundreds | Tens | Ones |
| | | |

Write the number.

3 hundreds

$$477 - 243$$

$$738 + 151$$

$$370 - 289$$

Frederick's shoelace broke into a 13-inch piece and a 27-inch piece. How long was his shoelace before it broke?

Color the greater number.

**400 + 30 + 9**

**300 + 40 + 9**

Which number sentence matches the picture?

○ 4 + 4 = 8

○ 6 + 2 = 8

○ 5 + 3 = 8

Subtract to find the missing numbers.

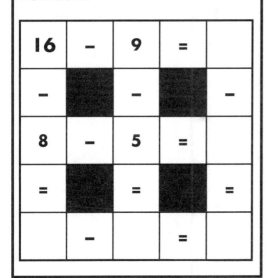

| 16 | – | 9 | = | |
|---|---|---|---|---|
| – | | – | | – |
| 8 | – | 5 | = | |
| = | | = | | = |
| | – | | = | |

**908 – 10 =**

Marty had 45 tennis balls. He hit 23 of them out of the court. How many balls does he have left?

Write the number.

six hundred fifty-one

_____ cm

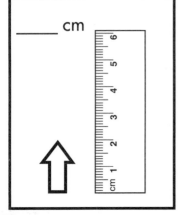

Write the numbers in expanded form.

**222 = _____**

**939 = _____**

The surf shop has 90 beach umbrellas. Sixty-one people rented umbrellas. How many beach umbrellas are left?

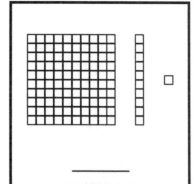

_____

**18 – 8 =**

◯ even

◯ odd

Draw base ten blocks to match the number.

**261**

| Number of Parked Cars | |
|---|---|
| Library | 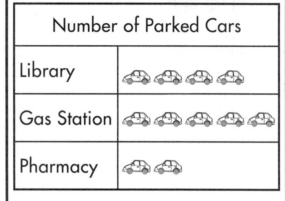 |
| Gas Station | |
| Pharmacy | |

🚗 = 1 car

How many cars are parked at the library? _____

How many more cars are at the gas station than the pharmacy?

_____

____ : ____

**14 + 3 =**

7 dimes and 1 quarter

_____ ¢

How much longer is one carrot than the other?

____ in.

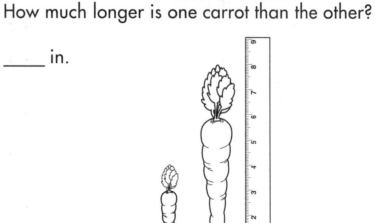

Draw a rectangular prism.

Marisa had $56. She spent $34 on groceries. How much money does she have left?

Write **<**, **>**, or **=** to compare.

356 ◯ 456

299 ◯ 280

545 ◯ 550

713 ◯ 703

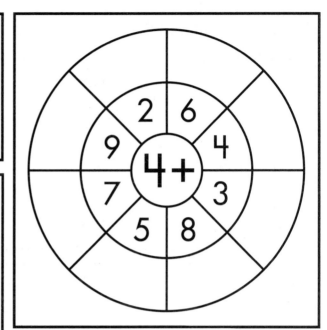

$$\begin{array}{r} 75 \\ -\ 29 \\ \hline \end{array}$$

$$\begin{array}{r} 34 \\ 56 \\ +\ 72 \\ \hline \end{array}$$

Color the shape that has an odd number of sides.

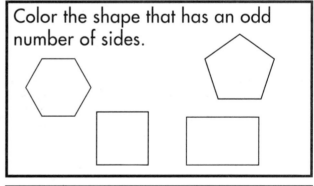

Which ice cream flavor do the most people like? _____

How many people like chocolate ice cream? _____

How many more people like vanilla than strawberry? _____

42, 52, _____, _____, _____

Which number sentence is true?

◯ 7 + 8 = 14      ◯ 9 + 3 = 13

◯ 6 + 7 = 12      ◯ 6 + 9 = 15

Match each time to the correct words.

| | |
|---|---|
| **7:15 am** | **seven fifteen in the evening** |
| **7:15 pm** | **midnight** |
| **12:00 am** | **seven fifteen in the morning** |
| **12:00 pm** | **noon** |

What are two ways to make $12 using only one- and five-dollar bills?

---

The pet store had 78 tropical fish. It sold 35 fish. Then the store got 42 more fish. How many fish does it have now?

◯ Addition only

◯ Subtraction only

◯ Addition and subtraction

**17 – 9 – 5 =**

Write a number sentence to match the array.

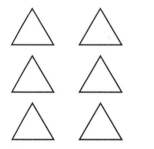

---

53
23
43
+ 63

Write 37 on the number line.

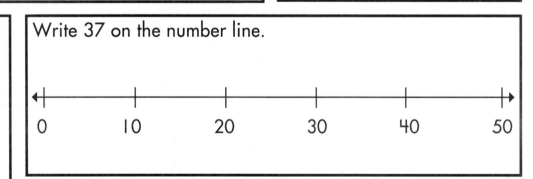

| 433 | | |
|---|---|---|
| Hundreds | Tens | Ones |
| | | |

**14 – 9 =**

**3 + 12 =**

Name _____

```
  98        53        47
- 76      - 29      - 18
```

Write the value of the underlined digit in each number.

4̲31 ____        5̲32 ____

8̲9 ____         38̲1 ____

Divide the rectangle into thirds.

Use drawings or words to explain how you would solve the problem.

42 – 11 = ____

The numbers in the squares are the sums of the numbers in the circles. Write the missing numbers.

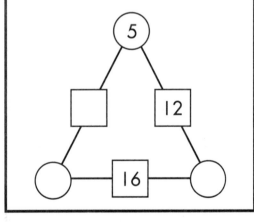

11 + 7 =

Write the number.

seven hundred forty-five

Grace has one window that is 45 in. wide and one window that is 36 in. wide. How much wider is the bigger window?

Draw dots to match the doubles fact.

3 + 3 = 6

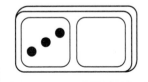

100 + 20 + 9 =

300 + 70 + 2 =

400 + 80 + 4 =

Arthur baked 24 muffins, 24 cupcakes, and 36 cookies. How many items did he bake?

Color one-fourth.

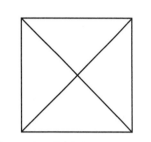

**15 + 2 =**

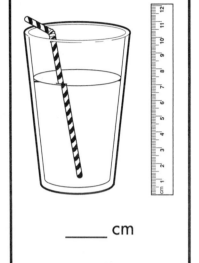

_____ cm

Skip count by 100 up the ladder.

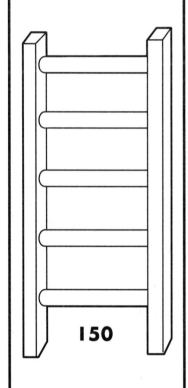

**150**

Draw a picture that uses at least one of each shape: circle, triangle, quadrilateral.

**607**

_____ hundreds

_____ tens

_____ ones

Draw two ways to make 46¢.

**312 + 10 =**

twelve forty

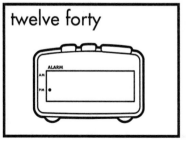

I have 6 faces. What am I?

◯ cube

◯ hexagon

◯ cylinder

An apple costs 60¢. A banana costs 35¢. How much more does the apple cost than the banana?

Which number sentence is not part of the fact family?

◯ 4 + 7 = 11

◯ 11 − 7 = 4

◯ 7 + 4 = 11

◯ 11 − 4 = 4

_____ + _____ + _____ + _____

= _____

670
+ 139

551
− 366

Write the missing numbers.

| | 56 | | |
|---|---|---|---|
| | | 67 | 68 |

434 − 100 =

Kendra has 23 blueberries and 15 strawberries. How many berries does she have?

Boats at the Dock

| Sailboat | 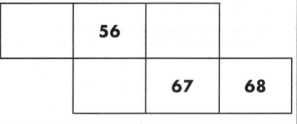 |
|---|---|
| Speedboat | |
| Fishing boat | |

△ = 1 boat

How many boats are at the dock? _____

Which boats are there equal numbers of at the dock? _____

How many more speedboats than sailboats are there? _____

Estimate the length of the rectangle.

_____ in.

Inches

0        1

---

**? – 34 = 61**

Which number sentence could you use to solve the problem?

○ 61 – 34
○ 61 + 34
○ 34 – 61
○ 34 + 34

---

| Musical Instruments Played | |
|---|---|
| Steven | ♩ ♩ ♩ |
| Violet | ♩ ♩ |
| Arnie | ♩ |
| Camille | ♩ ♩ ♩ ♩ |

Who plays 3 musical instruments? _____

How many more instruments does Camille play than Arnie? _____

---

**16 + 3 – 10 =**

---

Divide the rectangles into thirds two different ways.

---

$$\begin{array}{r} 8\ 7 \\ -\ 4\ \boxed{\phantom{0}} \\ \hline 4\ 1 \end{array}$$

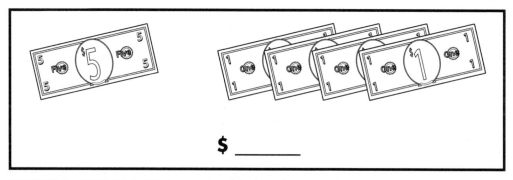

$ _____

---

Write the time words.

_____

---

Write **<**, **>**, or **=** to compare.

**571 ○ 561**

$$2\ 5$$
$$+\boxed{\ }4$$
$$\overline{8\ 9}$$

$$4\boxed{\ }$$
$$+3\ 4$$
$$\overline{7\ 6}$$

$$1\ 9$$
$$+\ 6\boxed{\ }$$
$$\overline{7\ 9}$$

Carlos has 35 feet of kite string. He needs 75 feet. How many more feet of kite string does he need?

$8 + 9 - 10 =$

Write a number sentence to match the picture.

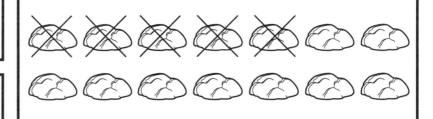

Circle each pair of numbers that equals 15. Some pairs are side by side and others are up and down.

| 8 | 7 | 1 | 3 | 9 | 4 |
|---|---|---|---|---|---|
| 2 | 5 | 10 | 8 | 6 | 11 |
| 12 | 7 | 4 | 13 | 2 | 5 |
| 3 | 11 | 9 | 6 | 14 | 8 |
| 10 | 5 | 1 | 12 | 1 | 0 |
| 8 | 6 | 7 | 4 | 9 | 15 |

$14 + 4 - 9 =$

Name the shape.

_____

How tall is the flagpole? _____ cm

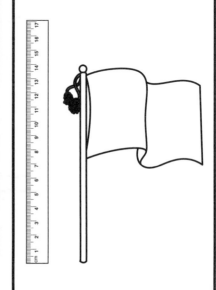

Draw an array to solve the problem.

$2 + 2 + 2 =$ ___

$$135$$
$$+\ 663$$

$$277$$
$$+\ 277$$

Muriel has 27 bottles of water. Arianna has 48. How many bottles do they have in all?

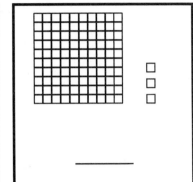

_____

15 – 12 =

Color an odd number of triangles.

45
+ ☐
–

24
+ ☐
–

86
+ ☐
–

31

**Shoe Size**

| x | | | | |
| x | x | | | |
| x | x | x | | |
| x | x | x | | x |
| **1** | **2** | **3** | **4** | **5** |

How many people wear shoe size 1? _____

How many more people wear size 2 than size 5? _____

How many people wear size 5 shoes? _____

**449**

_____ hundreds

_____ tens

_____ ones

12 + 8 =

three thirty-five

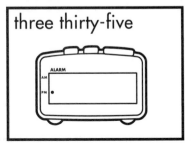

| Number Words | Hundreds _____ |
| | Tens _____ |
| **two hundred forty-two** | Ones _____ |
| Expanded Form | Base ten blocks |

How many sides does a hexagon have?

_____

Use addition to fill in the pyramid. Each number is the sum of the two numbers below it.

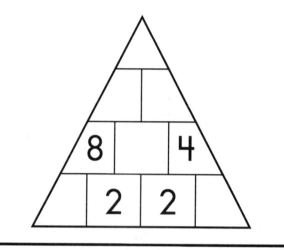

Ferdinand's deck is 13 feet long. Nancy's deck is 25 feet long. How many feet shorter is Ferdinand's deck?

Write **<**, **>**, or **=** to compare.

**377** ◯ **380**

**212** ◯ **221**

**414** ◯ **440**

**870** ◯ **910**

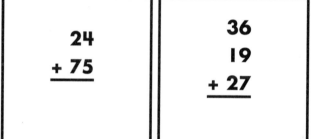

Write the number in words.

**129**

_____

_____

**555 – 100 = ____**

**6 + 10 – 8 + 5 =**

**Animals at the Farm**

How many more horses than pigs are at the farm? ____

How many more sheep than goats are there? ____

How many animals are at the farm? ____

Match the numbers.

306          300 + 60

316          300 + 6

360          300 + 60 + 1

361          300 + 10 + 6

Eddie had 46¢. Then, he found 1 quarter, 1 dime, and 13 pennies. How much money does he have now?

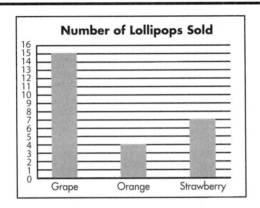

How many grape lollipops sold? _____

How many more strawberry than orange lollipops sold? _____

How many lollipops sold in all? _____

**7 hundreds + 5 ones = _____**

Draw a rectangle that can be divided into 8 square units.

· · · · · · ·

· · · · · · ·

· · · · · · ·

· · · · · · ·

· · · · · · ·

· · · · · · ·

32
58
23
+ 44

Which number sentence does the number line show?

○ 15 + 45          ○ 45 – 30          ○ 15 + 30

0  5  10  15  20  25  30  35  40  45  50

Write the time words.    8:20

Write **<**, **>**, or **=** to compare.

530 ◯ 529

76          56          39
+ 18        + 32        + 42

Luka has 5 dimes, 2 nickels, and 24 pennies. How much money does she have?

Circle the lesser number.

800 + 30 + 5

800 + 20 + 5

Circle the tree that has an even number of apples on it.

Add to find the missing numbers.

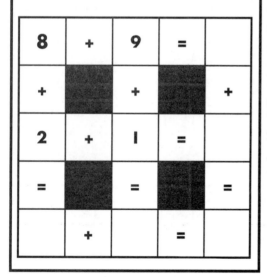

| 8 | + | 9 | = |   |
|---|---|---|---|---|
| + |   | + |   | + |
| 2 | + | 1 | = |   |
| = |   | = |   | = |
|   | + |   | = |   |

782 – 10 =

Write the number.

three hundred thirteen

Grayson has 49 feet of rope. He only needs 34 feet of rope. How many extra feet of rope does he have?

Write the doubles fact.

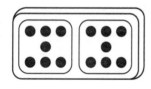

_____ + _____ = _____

47 – 22 =

◯ 22          ◯ 24

◯ 23          ◯ 25

Karissa had 64 craft sticks. She used 38 of them in an art project. How many does she have left?

82
− 64

14 − 12 =

_____ in.

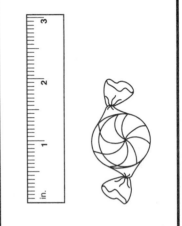

11 − 2 = ◯

◯ + 4 = ◯

◯ − ◯ = 2

8 + ◯ = ◯

15 − ◯ = ◯

8 + ◯ = 12

Label the three-dimensional shapes that you see in the castle.

_____ : _____

13 + 7 =

5 nickels and 3 dimes.

_____ ¢

Write **<**, **>**, or **=** to compare.

355 ◯ 360          244 ◯ 243

890 ◯ 880          555 ◯ 556

546 ◯ 456          342 ◯ 442

Divide the circle into thirds.

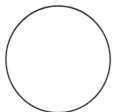

Draw an array to match the number sentence.

**3 + 3 + 3 + 3 + 3 = 15**

Write the fact family for the numbers.

**8      9      17**

____ + ____ = ____

____ + ____ = ____

____ - ____ = ____

____ - ____ = ____

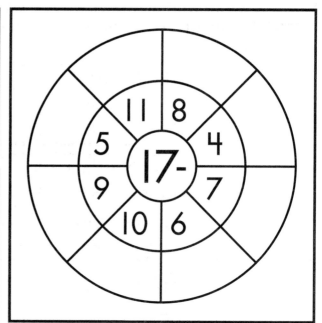

```
  344
+ 466
```

```
  35
  35
+ 35
```

Write the number in words.

**450**

_____

_____

450, 440, _____, _____, _____

| Number of Pizzas Made | |
|---|---|
| Cheese | 🍕🍕🍕🍕🍕🍕🍕🍕🍕 |
| Pepperoni | 🍕🍕🍕🍕🍕🍕🍕 |
| Vegetable | 🍕🍕🍕🍕🍕 |

🍕 = 2 pizzas

How many pepperoni pizzas were made?

____

How many more cheese than vegetable pizzas were made? ____

How many pizzas were made in all?

____

Jess counted 34 ants and 23 beetles. How many insects did she count in all?

Name _____

**Week 18, Day 3**

Measure the jar to the nearest inch and centimeter.

____ in.

____ cm

Yolanda had 36¢. She found 1 dime and 2 nickels between the couch cushions. How much money does she have now?

Number of Miles Run

```
                    x
            x       x
    x       x   x   x
    x       x   x   x   x
    _____
    1   2   3   4   5
```

How many people ran 2 miles? _____

What was the largest number of miles someone ran? _____

How many more people ran 3 miles than ran 1 mile? _____

$9 + 8 - 5 + 3 =$

Complete the number sentence for the array.

____ + ____ + ____ + ____

= 4

$$\begin{array}{r} 8\square \\ -\ 5\ 3 \\ \hline 3\ 6 \end{array}$$

Color the shape that has the greatest number of faces.

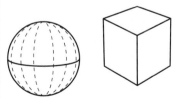   

**899**

| Hundreds | Tens | Ones |
|----------|------|------|
|          |      |      |

$7 + 3 =$

$8 + 4 =$

© Carson-Dellosa • CD-104882

87

| 746 | 277 | 399 |
|---|---|---|
| − 534 | + 219 | − 176 |

Lori had 67 mints. She ate some of them. Now she has 54 mints. How many mints did she eat?

599, _____, 601, _____,

_____

Cross out base ten blocks to subtract.

**437 − 316 = _____**

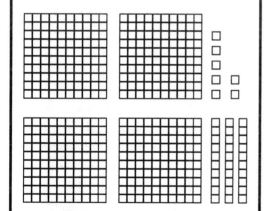

○ even     ○ odd

**19 − 13 =**

Write the number.

nine hundred seventy

How much longer is one marker than the other?

_____ in.

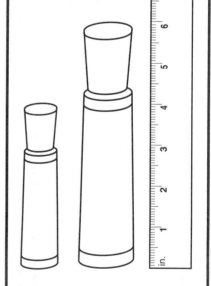

Complete the doubles fact.

_____ + _____ = 16

Write the numbers in expanded form.

**460 = _____**

**399 = _____**

There were 54 people at the grocery store. Some people left. Twenty-six more people came into the store. Then, there were 67 people at the grocery store. How many people left?

How much is shaded? _____

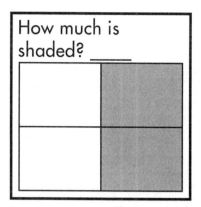

10 + 503 =

Estimate the length of the butterfly in centimeters.

_____ cm

centimeters
0                    1
|ııııı|ıııı|

Count by 5s to fill in the missing ladder rungs.

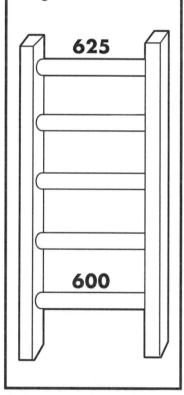

**625**

**600**

700 – 100 =

6 dimes and 36 pennies

_____ ¢

**Students' Favorite Transportation**

8
6
4
2
0
Car    Bus    Train    Airplane

How many students prefer to travel by airplane? _____

How many more students prefer a car to a bus? _____

How many students prefer to travel by train? _____

Show 4:55.

Measure the straw to the nearest inch and centimeter.
_____ in.

_____ cm

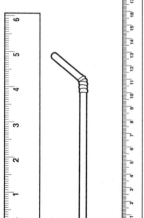

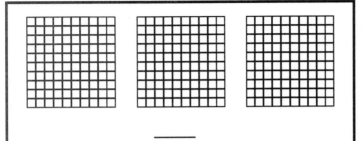

_____

Draw an array for the number sentence.

$$4 + 4 + 4 = 12$$

Janis had 70 in. of aluminum foil. She used 23 in. to wrap up food. How many in. does she have left?

Write **<**, **>**, or **=** to compare.

455 ◯ 555

323 ◯ 323

247 ◯ 237

110 ◯ 110

437
+ 388
_____

36
84
+ 29
_____

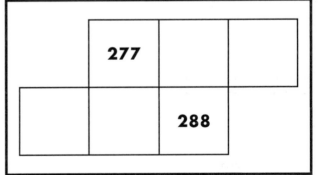

696, 596, _____, _____, _____

| Slices of Pizzas Eaten | |
|---|---|
| Marty | 🍕 🍕 |
| Elena | 🍕 🍕 |
| Ursula | 🍕 🍕 🍕 🍕 |
| Figaro | 🍕 🍕 🍕 |

🍕 = 1 slice

Who ate the most pizza? _____

Which people ate the same amount of pizza? _____

How many slices were eaten in all? _____

$$15 - 7 + 5 + 6 =$$

_____ cm

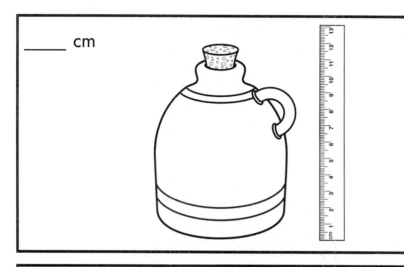

Annette's table is 45 in. long. Her tablecloth is 78 in. long. How much longer is the tablecloth than the table?

Orville bought 70 shrimp and 20 oysters at the fish market. He used 48 pieces of seafood in a recipe. How many pieces of seafood does he have left?

○ addition only

○ addition and subtraction

○ subtraction only

**20 − 12 + 6 + 1 =**

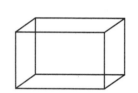

○ rectangle

○ cube

○ prism

33
44
55
+ 66

Use the number line to show the problem.

**35 − 7 = 28**

20        25        30        35        40

Write the time in words.

18 − 16 =

15 + 3 =

$$\begin{array}{r} \boxed{\phantom{0}}6 \\ +\ 4\ 3 \\ \hline 8\ 9 \end{array}$$
$$\begin{array}{r} 2\ 8 \\ +7\boxed{\phantom{0}} \\ \hline 9\ 9 \end{array}$$
$$\begin{array}{r} 5\ 2 \\ +3\boxed{\phantom{0}} \\ \hline 9\ 0 \end{array}$$

Write the value of the 8 in each number.

508 _____        283 _____

877 _____        980 _____

Write <, >, or = to compare.

**340 ◯ 339**

Write a number sentence for the problem shown. Then, solve it.

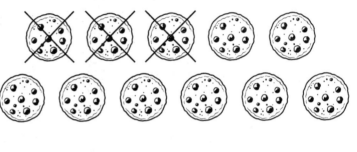

The numbers in the squares are the sums of the numbers in the circles. Write the missing numbers.

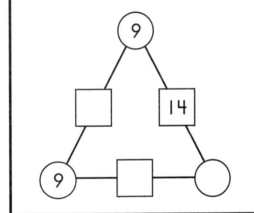

**920 – 100 =**

Write the number.

two hundred two

Victor had $20. He spent a $5 bill and three $1 bills. How much money does he have left?

A chair would most likely be _____ tall.

◯ 1 inch

◯ 1 centimeter

◯ 1 yard

$$\begin{array}{r} 6\ 8 \\ -\ 4\ 9 \\ \hline \end{array}$$
$$\begin{array}{r} 7\ 6 \\ -\ 5\ 5 \\ \hline \end{array}$$

Maureen had 24 glasses. She broke some glasses. She bought 12 more. Now she has 28 glasses. How many did she break?

---

23
+ 65

---

15 – 14 =

---

Color an even number of spoons.

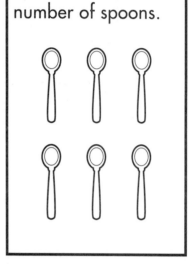

---

Write the missing number and circle the operations to get from 76 to 69.

76
+
–
☐

52
+
–
☐

21
+
–
☐

69

---

Banana Lengths in Inches

```
          x
          x
          x
 x    x          x
 x    x    x    x    x
 x    x    x    x    x
 6    7    8    9    10
```

How long were the shortest bananas measured? _____

What was the measurement with the most bananas? _____

How many bananas were measured in all? _____

---

Show 4:35.

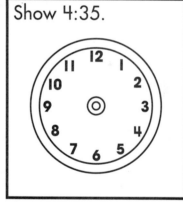

---

334 + 10 =

---

5 nickels, 1 dime, and 1 penny

_____ ¢

---

| Number Words | Hundreds _____ |
| --- | --- |
| | Tens _____ |
| | Ones _____ |
| Expanded Form  100 + 80 + 5 | Base Ten Blocks |

Divide the rectangle into 10 equal parts.

Draw an array for the number sentence.

**3 + 3 + 3 = 9**

David had 68¢. He dropped a quarter and lost it. How much money does he have left?

Which number sentence does not belong in the fact family?

◯ 3 + 8 = 11

◯ 11 − 3 = 8

◯ 8 + 3 = 11

◯ 8 − 11 = 3

$$\begin{array}{r} 91 \\ -\ 57 \\ \hline \end{array}$$

$$\begin{array}{r} 65 \\ 32 \\ +\ 19 \\ \hline \end{array}$$

Write the number in words.

**565**

_____

_____

782, 781, _____, _____, _____

How many in. longer is one pen than the other?

_____ in.

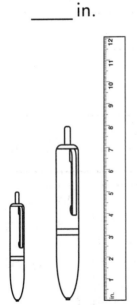

**16 − 12 + 9 − 7 =**

Match the expanded form to the number word.

300 + 40 + 9     **three hundred ninety-four**

300 + 4          **three hundred forty-nine**

300 + 9          **three hundred four**

300 + 90 + 4     **three hundred nine**

---

Shelby has 35 markers and 42 crayons. How many coloring tools does she have altogether?

---

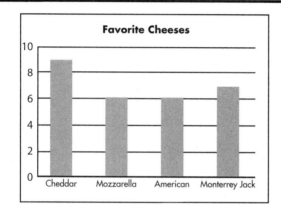

How many people prefer Monterrey Jack cheese? _____

How many more people prefer cheddar than mozzarella? _____

---

6 + 10 − 4 =

---

Draw a rectangle that can be divided into 6 equal parts.

. . . . . .

. . . . . .

. . . . . .

. . . . . .

. . . . . .

---

76
33
81
+ 64

---

What does  represent? _____

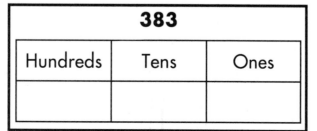

---

**383**

| Hundreds | Tens | Ones |
|----------|------|------|
|          |      |      |

---

Write **<**, **>**, or **=** to compare.

**609** ◯ **709**

Jacob had 54 pieces of licorice. He gave 24 pieces to his friends. Then, he ate 7 pieces. How many pieces of licorice does he have left?

Write the value of the underlined digit in each number.

5**5**5 ____        **3**30 ____

82**0** ____        **2**09 ____

Circle the greater number.

700 + 80 + 9

700 + 90

Is the number of shaded circles even or odd?

○ even     ○ odd

Cross out base ten blocks to subtract.

**259 – 157 = ____**

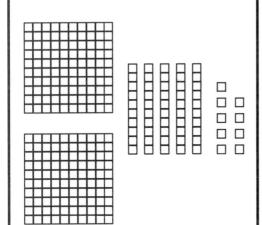

**983 – 10 =**

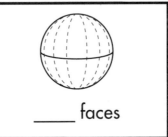

____ faces

Carly had 1 nickel, 1 dime, and 43 pennies. Then she found 1 quarter. How much money does she have now?

Write the doubles fact.

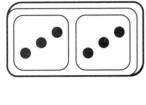

____ + ____ = ____

| 377 | 626 |
|---|---|
| + 299 | + 108 |

Natalia had 45 gallons of water. She used 10 gallons to make lemonade. How many gallons of water does she have left?

_____ hundred

_____ ten

**17 + 3 =**

Color an even number of circles.

18 – 9 = ◯
↓
17 – ◯ = ◯
↓
12 – ◯ = ◯
↓
11 – ◯ = ◯
↓
15 – ◯ = ◯
↓
16 – 8 = ◯

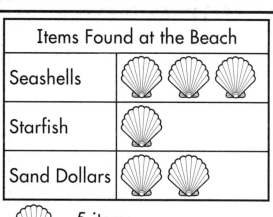

| Items Found at the Beach | |
|---|---|
| Seashells | 🐚 🐚 🐚 |
| Starfish | 🐚 |
| Sand Dollars | 🐚 🐚 |

🐚 = 5 items

How many more seashells than starfish were found? _____

How many sand dollars were found? _____

How many items were found in all? _____

_____ : _____

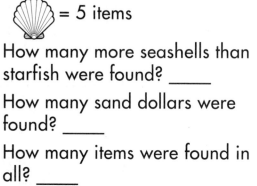

**176 – 100 =**

Measure the piece of string to the nearest inch and centimeter.

_____ in.     _____ cm

in. 1  2  3  4  5  6  7  8  9  10  11  12

cm 1 2 3 4 5 6 7 8 9 10 11 12 13 14 15 16 17

4 dimes and 7 nickels

_____ ¢

How is the circle divided?

○ halves

○ thirds

○ fourths

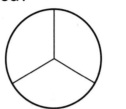

Hannah had 98¢. She spent 2 quarters and a dime on a pack of gum. How much money does she have left?

Write **<**, **>**, or **=** to compare.

**797** ○ **790**

**380** ○ **370**

**422** ○ **522**

**337** ○ **338**

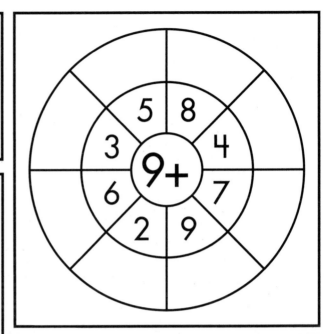

```
  89
- 67
____
```

```
  14
  54
+ 34
____
```

Write the number in words.

**360**

_____

_____

718, 708, _____, _____, _____

**17 + 3 − 10 + 4 =**

| Glasses of Water | |
|---|---|
| Stephen | 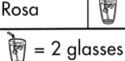 |
| Maria | |
| Eli | |
| Rosa | |

= 2 glasses

Who drank the most water? _____

How many glasses of water were drunk in all? _____

Which people drank the same amount of water? _____

Match the time in words to the time shown.

three fifteen in the morning     7:50 am

three fifty in the morning     7:15 pm

three fifteen in the afternoon     7:50 pm

three fifty in the afternoon     7:15 am

---

**73 − ✦ = 45**

Which number sentence could you use to solve the problem?

○ 73 + 45 = ✦

○ 45 − 73 = ✦

○ 73 − 45 = ✦

---

Use the tally chart to fill in the line plot.

| Servings of Fruit Eaten | |
|---|---|
| 1 serving | I I I I |
| 2 servings | I I I |
| 3 servings | I I |
| 4 servings | I I |

Servings of Fruit Eaten

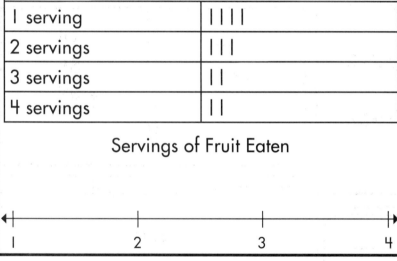

1      2      3      4

---

**3 hundreds + 9 tens = _____**

---

I have 5 faces, 8 edges, and 5 vertices. What am I?

_____

---

23
32
45
+ 54

---

10¢ 10¢ 10¢ 10¢ 10¢ 10¢ 10¢

1¢ 1¢ 1¢ 1¢ 1¢      _____ ¢

---

**701**

| Hundreds | Tens | Ones |
|---|---|---|
| | | |

---

**14 + 6 =**

**9 − 8 =**

| 68 | 37 | 26 |
|---|---|---|
| + 24 | + 38 | + 59 |

What is the value of the underlined digit?

**3<u>9</u>8**

- ○ 9
- ○ 90
- ○ 900

Circle the greater number.

seven hundred seven

seven hundred seventy

Use a picture or words to explain how you solve the problem.

**24 – 19 =**

Circle each pair of numbers whose sum is 16. Some pairs are side by side and others are up and down.

| 1 | 12 | 3 | 6 | 12 | 4 |
|---|---|---|---|---|---|
| 15 | 1 | 7 | 10 | 3 | 10 |
| 4 | 8 | 5 | 1 | 14 | 9 |
| 7 | 8 | 16 | 9 | 7 | 13 |
| 2 | 14 | 0 | 13 | 8 | 3 |
| 8 | 5 | 9 | 5 | 11 | 4 |

**433 + 10 =**

Write the number.

five hundred fifty-five

The smoothie stand has 36 flavors of smoothies and 25 flavors of milkshakes. How many drink choices are there in all?

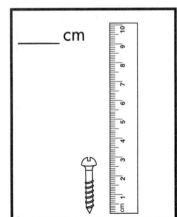

_____ cm

| 91 | 57 |
|---|---|
| – 48 | – 39 |

Hunter has 48 shirts. 26 of them are T-shirts. How many are not T-shirts?

$$\begin{array}{r} 90 \\ -\ 58 \\ \hline \end{array}$$

226 + 10 =

What is the best estimate for the height of a table?

○ 1 inch

○ 1 meter

○ 1 centimeter

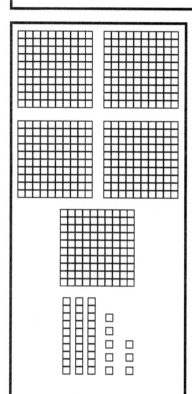

_____

Write the name of each shape.

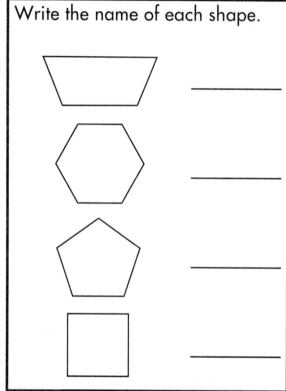

_____

_____

_____

_____

668

_____ hundreds

_____ tens

_____ ones

4 + 7 − 3 =

three twenty

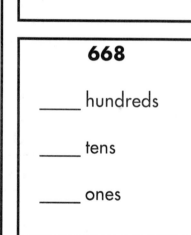

Draw two ways to make 42¢.

Divide the squares into fourths three different ways.

Use addition to fill in the pyramid. Each number is the sum of the two numbers below it.

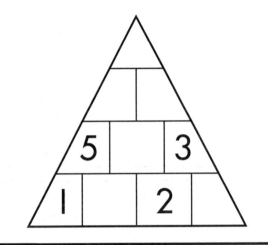

Write a number sentence for the array.

Complete the fact family.

____ + 1 = 7

1 + 6 = ____

7 - ____ = 6

____ - 6 = 1

| 346 | 709 |
| + 289 | - 455 |

Write the missing numbers.

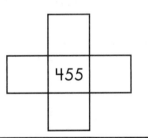

455

How much taller is one tulip than the other?

____ cm

778 - 100 = ____

Which number sentence is true?

◯ 6 + 1 = 8      ◯ 4 + 3 = 6

◯ 5 - 1 = 4      ◯ 7 - 1 = 5

_____ in.

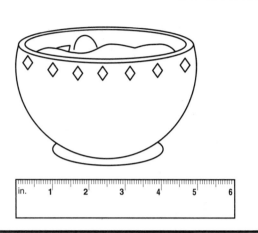

Karissa had 40¢. She found a nickel and 8 pennies on the sidewalk. How much money does she have now?

---

Finn made 90 mini sandwiches for a party. His guests ate 69 mini sandwiches. Then, he gave 12 to his sister. How many mini sandwiches does he have left?

Which number sentence could you use to solve the problem?

○ **90 – 69 + 12**

○ **90 – 69 – 12**

○ **90 – 12 + 69**

○ **90 + 69 + 12**

---

**17 – 9 + 7 – 6 =**

---

Draw a rectangle that can be divided into 20 square units.

```
.   .   .   .   .   .   .
.   .   .   .   .   .   .
.   .   .   .   .   .   .
.   .   .   .   .   .   .
.   .   .   .   .   .   .
.   .   .   .   .   .   .
```

---

```
  4 8 9
-  1 □ 6
  3 3 3
```

Use the number line to show the problem.

**45 – 25 = 20**

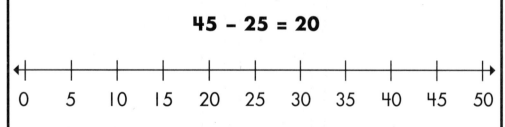

Write the time in words.

_____

Write **<**, **>**, or **=** to compare.

**888** ◯ **988**

46     5☐     ☐3
-☐1    -17    -42
15     41     31

Grady has 35 red marbles, 22 purple marbles, and 31 green marbles. How many marbles does he have in all?

Which shape is a quadrilateral?

○ trapezoid    ○ pentagon

○ triangle

Write a number sentence to match the picture.

The numbers in the squares are the sums of the numbers in the circles. Write the missing numbers.

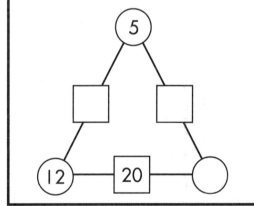

671 + 10 =

Write the number.

seven hundred ninety-nine

Magdalena has 36 shoes. Eighteen of them are sandals. How many are not sandals?

Write the doubles fact.

___ + ___ = ___

Write each numbers in expanded form.

306 = _____

228 = _____

Corinna has 14 dolls and 28 stuffed animals. How many toys does she have in all?

Divide the rectangle into triangular halves.

15 – 11 =

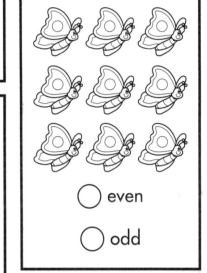

◯ even

◯ odd

Count by 10s up the ladder.

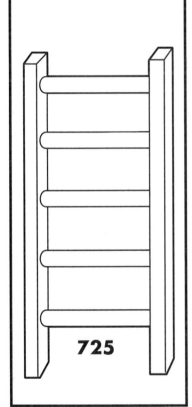

**725**

**Favorite Pizza Topping**

12
11
10
9
8
7
6
5
4
3
2
1
0
Pepperoni   Olives   Peppers   Sausage

Which pizza topping is 7 peoples' favorite? _____

How many more people prefer pepperoni than sausage? ____

How many people prefer peppers? ____

Show 7:05.

342 – 100 =

1 quarter and 6 dimes

_____ ¢

Number Words

Hundreds ____

Tens ____

Ones ____

Expanded Form

Base Ten Blocks

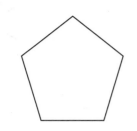

_____ sides

_____ angles

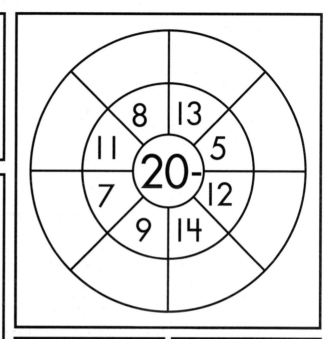

The library has a flagpole that is 15 feet tall. The fire station has one that is 22 feet tall. How much taller is the fire station's flagpole?

Write **<**, **>**, or **=** to compare.

644 ◯ 633

272 ◯ 270

399 ◯ 599

405 ◯ 415

81
- 29
_____

25
36
+ 47
_____

Write the number in words.

**505**

_____

_____

651, 650, _____, _____, _____

Measure the mug to the nearest centimeter and inch.

_____ in.

_____ cm

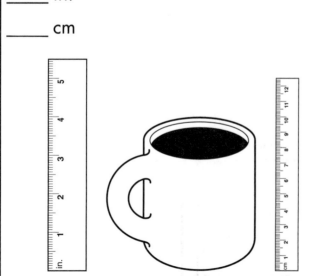

Kyle has 67 frogs and 23 fish in his pond. How many more frogs than fish are there?

Match each shape to the number of faces, edges, or vertices.

| | |
|---|---|
| **cone** | **5 faces** |
| **cylinder** | **1 vertex** |
| **pyramid** | **12 edges** |
| **cube** | **no vertices** |

Ray had $15. He made $20 mowing his neighbor's lawn. How much money does he have now?

| Books Read in One Month | |
|---|---|
| Julia | ▯▯▯▯▯▯▯▯▯▯ |
| Cameron | ▯▯▯▯▯ |
| Heath | ▯▯▯▯▯▯ |
| Bianca | ▯▯▯ |

▯ = 1 book

How many more books did Julia read than Heath? ____

Who read five books? ____

How many books were read in all? ____

**14 − 7 − 4 + 9 =**

Write a number sentence to match the array.

```
  48
  22
  39
+ 55
```

25¢     10¢ 10¢ 10¢     1¢ 1¢

_____ ¢

| 664 | | |
|---|---|---|
| Hundreds | Tens | Ones |
| | | |

**3 + 17 =**

**2 + 11 =**

33        72        61
+ 58      - 54      - 38

Bella knitted 23 scarves last year. She has knitted 14 scarves this year. How many scarves has she knitted in all?

Write <, >, or = to compare.

522 ◯ 512

How many people prefer macaroni?

_____

How many more people prefer ravioli than spaghetti? _____

How many people have a favorite pasta dish? _____

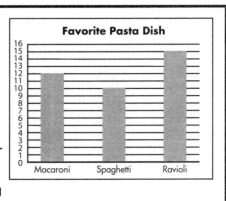

**Favorite Pasta Dish**

Macaroni    Spaghetti    Ravioli

Subtract to find the missing numbers.

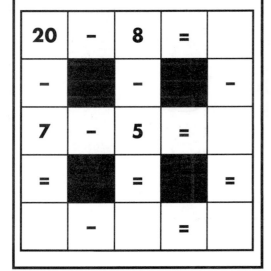

| 20 | – | 8 | = | |
|----|---|---|---|---|
| – | | – | | – |
| 7 | – | 5 | = | |
| = | | = | | = |
| | – | | = | |

700 – 10 =

Write the number.

five hundred fifty-three

_____

Write the doubles fact.

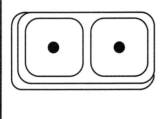

____ + ____ = ____

38 – 14 =

◯ 23        ◯ 25

◯ 24        ◯ 26

_____ cm

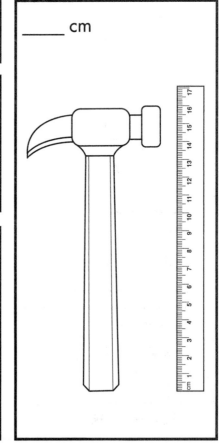

Rudy had 72 crayons. He broke 19 of them. How many whole crayons does he have left?

34
+ 36

320 + 100 =

_____ cm

Write the numbers and circle the operations to get from 23 to 42.

**23**

+
–

**37**

+
–

**11**

+
–

**42**

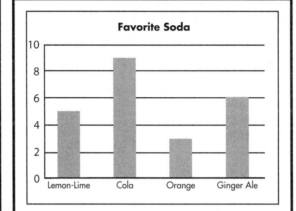

**Favorite Soda**

How many more people prefer cola than orange soda? _____
How many more people prefer ginger ale than lemon-lime soda?

_____

How many people have a favorite soda? _____

**344**

____ hundreds

____ tens

____ ones

782 – 100 =

six forty-five

Write **<**, **>**, or **=** to compare.

256 ◯ 266          301 ◯ 305

387 ◯ 487          644 ◯ 634

499 ◯ 499          708 ◯ 808

_____

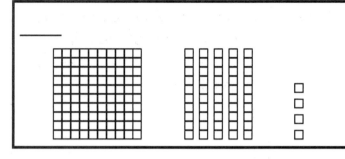

Sierra has 4 dimes, a nickel, and 28 pennies. How much money will she have left if she spends 35¢?

Which number sentence is not part of the fact family?

○ 2 + 4 = 6

○ 4 + 2 = 6

○ 6 – 4 = 2

○ 2 – 6 = 4

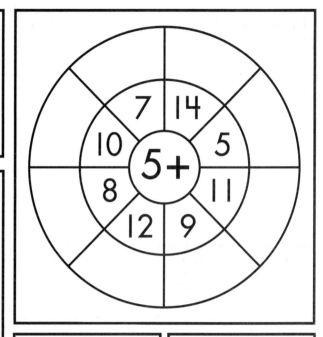

5 +
7  14
10      5
8      11
12  9

708
– 355

77
33
+ 26

How much taller is one plant than the other?

_____ in.

Color the ice cream cone that has an even number of sprinkles

203, 202, _____, _____,

2 + 13 – 4 + 6 =

How much longer is one pencil than the other?

_____ cm

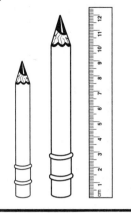

Erin had 87 chocolate chips. She used 66 of them in a recipe. How many does she have left?

**Students' Favorite Toys**

How many students prefer board games? _____

How many more students prefer stuffed animals than cars? _____

What toy is the most students' favorite? _____

**3 hundreds + 6 tens**

**= _____**

Divide the rectangle into two rows and four columns. How many pieces are there?

```
  39
  22
  81
+ 55
```

What does ☆ represent on the number line? _____

40 41 42 43 44 45 46 47 48 49 50 51 52 53 54 55 56 ☆ 58 59 60

The animal shelter has 45 cats and 50 dogs. How many animals are there?

16 – 14 =

13 + 1 =

Rachael made 80 pies for her bakery. Some pies sold, so she made 25 more. Now she has 67 pies in her bakery. How many sold?

Write the value of the underlined digit.

**77**1 ____          **669** ____

**77**0 ____          **668** ____

Circle the lesser number.

300 + 40

300 + 9

Draw a picture or use words to explain how you solved the problem.

**24 + 18 = ____**

Cross out base ten blocks to subtract.

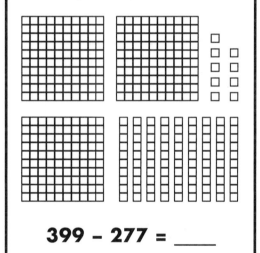

**399 – 277 = ____**

**767 – 100 =**

Write the number.

nine hundred one

Ariel collected 26 shells on Monday and 39 shells on Tuesday. On Wednesday, she gave 18 shells to Mia. How many shells did she have left?

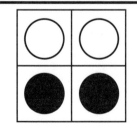

____ + ____ = ____

```
  409          322
- 277        + 556
-----        -----
```

Erika has 27 carrot sticks and 27 celery sticks. How many veggie sticks does she have?

Color one half of each square.

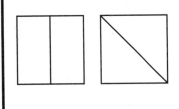

**346 + 10 =**

Color an even number of candies.

7 + 3 = ◯

◯ + 4 = ◯

◯ + ◯ = 8

9 + ◯ = ◯

◯ + 3 = ◯

◯ + 7 = 15

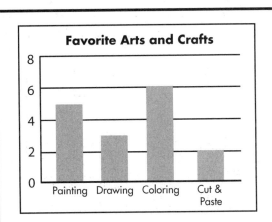

**Favorite Arts and Crafts**

How many more people prefer painting than drawing? _____

How many people prefer coloring? _____

How many more people prefer coloring than cut & paste? _____

Show 9:35.

How long is the dollar bill? _____ in.

**506 – 10 =**

56 pennies and 5 nickels

_____ ¢

____ faces

____ edges

____ vertices

Ricky's ladder is 18 feet tall. Doug's ladder is 26 feet tall. How much taller is Doug's ladder than Ricky's?

Complete the fact family.

____ + 8 = 10

8 + 2 = ____

10 − ____ = 2

____ − 2 = 8

Use addition to fill in the pyramid. Each number is the sum of the two numbers below it.

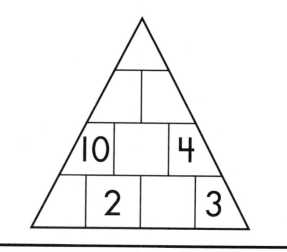

$$\begin{array}{r} 270 \\ + 459 \\ \hline \end{array}$$

$$\begin{array}{r} 800 \\ - 462 \\ \hline \end{array}$$

Write the missing numbers.

| 887 | |
|-----|-----|
| | 898 |

**999 − 100 = ____**

**19 − 5 − 7 − 3 =**

____ cm

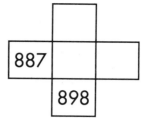

Measure the cotton swab to the nearest inch and centimeter.

_____ in.

_____ cm

Victoria had 2 quarters, 3 dimes, and 3 nickels. She put 50¢ into a parking meter. How much money does she have left?

Use the tally chart to complete the line plot.

| Length of Pencils | |
|---|---|
| 3 in. | I I I |
| 4 in. | I I I I |
| 5 in. | I I I I |
| 6 in. | I I |

Length of Pencils

```
←+————————+————————+————————+→
 3        4        5        6
```

**9 hundreds + 3 ones**
**= _____**

Divide the rectangle into 2 rows and 3 columns. How many squares are there?

_____

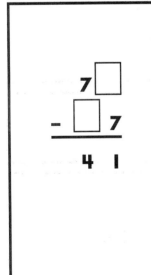

Which number sentence does the number line show?

◯ **60 + 90**          ◯ **90 – 60**          ◯ **90 – 30**

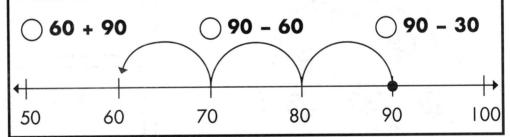

Write the time in words.

_____

**252 + 100 =**

**115**

460     279     443
- 338   - 86   - 271

Caroline has 88 meters of yarn. Jessica has 61 meters of yarn. How many fewer meters does Jessica have?

Circle the lesser number.

one hundred thirty

seventy-nine

The numbers in the squares are the sums of the numbers in the circles. Write the missing numbers.

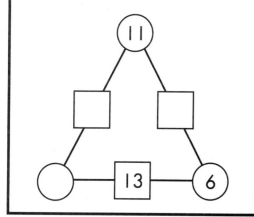

◯ even     ◯ odd

545 – 10 =

Write the number.

eight hundred fourteen

Charlie has 3 dimes and 7 pennies. Lucy has 4 nickels and 12 pennies. Who has more money?

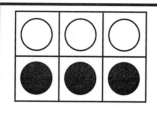

____ + ____

= ____

500 + 50 + 3 = ____

200 + 40 + 2 = ____

700 + 80 = ____

600 + 1 = ____

The computer's screen is 13 inches. The television's screen is 40 inches. How much wider is the television's screen?

$$82$$
$$- 67$$

381 + 10 =

_____ cm

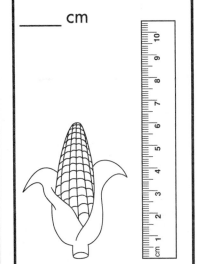

Write the numbers and circle the operations to get from 43 to 21.

**43**

+ [ ]
−

**68**

+ [ ]
−

**41**

+ [ ]
−

**21**

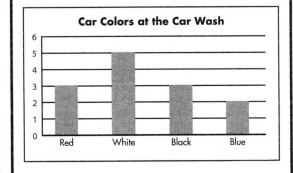

**Car Colors at the Car Wash**

How many more white cars than blue cars were at the car wash?

_____

How many red and black cars were there? _____

How many cars were at the car wash in all? _____

**500**

_____ hundreds

_____ tens

_____ ones

13 − 9 + 8 =

3 quarters and 18 pennies

_____ ¢

| Number Words | Hundreds: **2** |
| | Tens: **6** |
| | One: **2** |
| Expanded Form | Base Ten Blocks |

Draw an array to match the number sentence.

$$4 + 4 = 8$$

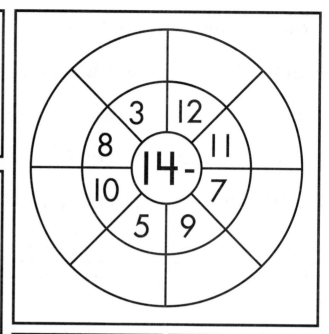

Misty had 25 pillows. She got some more pillows. Now she has 39 pillows. How many did she get?

Write **<**, **>**, or **=** to compare.

810 ◯ 808

435 ◯ 440

366 ◯ 266

812 ◯ 813

$$\begin{array}{r} 606 \\ -\ 333 \\ \hline \end{array}$$

$$\begin{array}{r} 34 \\ 62 \\ +\ 77 \\ \hline \end{array}$$

Write the number in words.

**602**

_____

_____

Measure the candle to the nearest inch and centimeter.

_____ in.

_____ cm

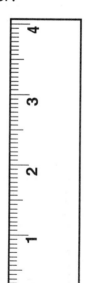

733, 723, _____, _____, _____

Ingrid has 78 crayons. There are 24 green ones. How many are not green?

Match the expanded form to the number word.

600 + 20 + 1          **six hundred twenty-two**

600 + 20 + 2          **six hundred twelve**

600 + 10 + 2          **six hundred eleven**

600 + 10 + 1          **six hundred twenty-one**

---

Adam had 64¢. He found a quarter and 3 pennies. How much money does he have now?

---

Which number sentence could you use to solve the problem?

Beth had 40 lollipops. She gave 20 to her cousins. Then she bought 14 more lollipops. How many does she have now?

○ 40 – 20 – 14

○ 20 + 14 + 40

○ 40 – 20 + 14

○ 20 – 14 + 40

---

3 + 10 + 7 – 9 =

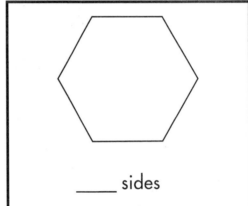

_____ sides

_____ angles

---

32
44
19
+ 25

---

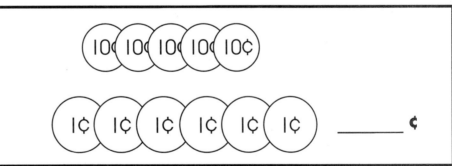

_____ ¢

---

Write the time words.

_____

---

18 – 6 =

14 – 5 =

```
  8 9        6 □        □ 6
- 3 □      - 2 4      - 2 3
  5 2        4 3        5 3
```

Beatrice has 14 folding chairs. Teddy has 16 folding chairs. How many chairs do they have altogether?

Circle the greater number.

$900 + 70 + 1$

$900 + 10 + 7$

Write a number sentence to match the picture.

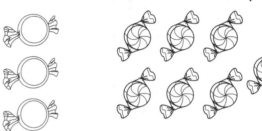

Add to find the missing numbers.

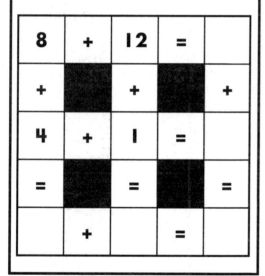

| 8 | + | 12 | = | |
| + | | + | | + |
| 4 | + | 1 | = | |
| = | | = | | = |
| | + | | = | |

$239 + 10 =$

Write the number.

five hundred five

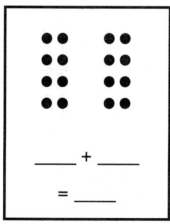

```
  209        645
+ 392      + 112
```

____ + ____

= ____

_____ cm

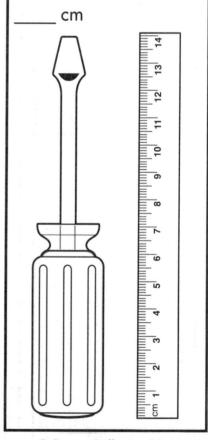

Melissa and Joey have 45 cherries. They eat 28 cherries. How many cherries are left?

How much is shaded? _____

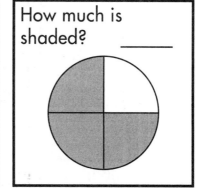

**786 + 100 =**

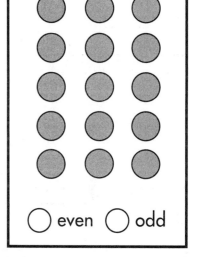

◯ even  ◯ odd

Count by 10s down the ladder.

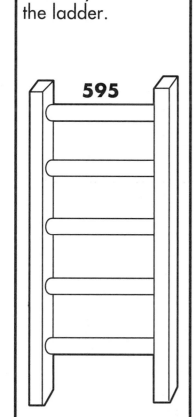

**595**

| Family Vehicles | |
|---|---|
| Car | 🛞 🛞 🛞 🛞 🛞 🛞 |
| Van | 🛞 🛞 🛞 🛞 |
| Truck | 🛞 🛞 🛞 |

🛞 = 5 families

How many more families drive cars than trucks? _____

How many families drive vans?

_____

_____ : _____

**662 – 10 =**

3 nickels and 63 pennies

_____ ¢

Write **<**, **>**, or **=** to compare.

89 ◯ 809          124 ◯ 125

314 ◯ 159          308 ◯ 308

602 ◯ 236          535 ◯ 585

Divide the rectangle into 9 columns. How many pieces are there? _____

[empty rectangle]

The fruit stand had 54 melons. 18 melons sold in the morning. 27 melons sold in the afternoon. How many melons were left at the end of the day?

Which number sentence does not belong in the fact family?

○ 2 + 8 = 10

○ 8 + 10 = 18

○ 10 − 8 = 2

○ 10 − 2 = 8

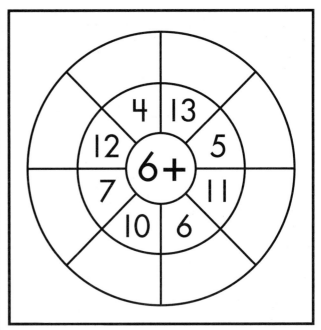

$$\begin{array}{r} 108 \\ + 229 \\ \hline \end{array}$$

$$\begin{array}{r} 28 \\ 64 \\ + 19 \\ \hline \end{array}$$

Write the missing numbers.

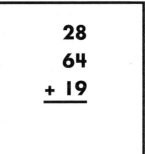

347

337 + 100 = _____

17 − 7 − 5 + 8 =

**Favorite Outdoor Activity**

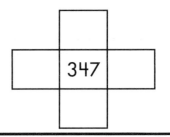

How many more people prefer biking than rollerblading? _____

How many more people prefer skateboarding than jumping rope? _____

Estimate the length of the potato in inches.

_____ in.

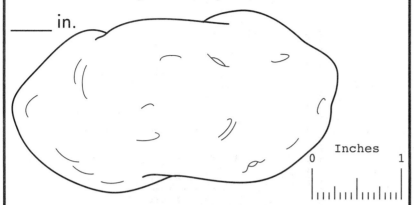

Inches
0                    1

---

$46 -$ ✵ $= 32$
Which number sentence could you use to solve the problem?

○ $32 - 46 =$ ✵

○ $46 - 32 =$ ✵

○ $32 + 32 =$ ✵

---

Use the information from the tally chart to complete the line plot.

| Lengths of Necklaces | |
|---|---|
| 16 inches | 卌 \|\|\| |
| 18 inches | 卌 |
| 20 inches | \|\|\|\| |

Lengths of Necklaces

16        17        18        19        20

---

$13 + 5 - 9 + 2 =$ _____

---

Color in three fourths of each square.

---

Write **40** on the number line.

0                                                                50

---

30
50
20
+ 45

---

| 460 | | |
|---|---|---|
| Hundreds | Tens | Ones |
| | | |

---

$7 + 11 =$

$18 - 14 =$

```
  544        605        342
+ 388      - 470      + 612
```

Steve had 84 pieces of bread. He made sandwiches with 46 of the pieces. How many pieces were left?

13 – 3 – 4 + 5 =

12 + 7 – 2 – 6 =

Which activity is 9 people's favorite?

_____

_____

How many more people like sledding?

_____

How many more people prefer building a snowman than making snow angels? _____

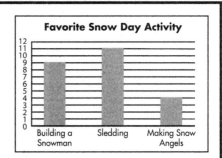

**Favorite Snow Day Activity**

Circle each pair of numbers that equals 14. Some pairs are side by side, and others are up and down.

| 8 | 9 | 6 | 2 | 4 | 7 |
|---|---|---|---|---|---|
| 3 | 11 | 1 | 12 | 5 | 7 |
| 4 | 6 | 8 | 9 | 0 | 14 |
| 9 | 7 | 2 | 3 | 10 | 5 |
| 5 | 1 | 13 | 7 | 4 | 2 |
| 10 | 8 | 5 | 1 | 7 | 6 |

210 + 100 =

Name the shape.

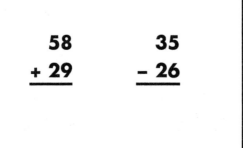

Anita had $5 and 36¢. She spent $3 and one quarter. How much money does she have left?

○ even  ○ odd

```
  58        35
+ 29      - 26
```

Jordan has 14 cousins that are boys and 16 cousins that are girls. How many cousins does she have?

43
+ 19

518 – 100 =

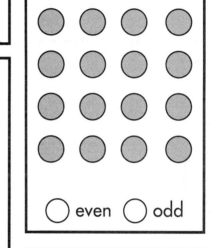

◯ even   ◯ odd

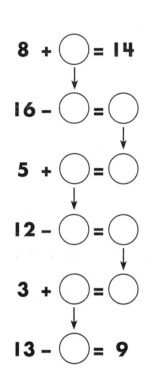

8 + ◯ = 14

16 – ◯ = ◯

5 + ◯ = ◯

12 – ◯ = ◯

3 + ◯ = ◯

13 – ◯ = 9

**Favorite Fair Ride**

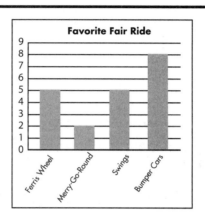

How many more people prefer bumper cars than the merry-go-round? ____

How many people prefer the Ferris wheel? ____

How many people prefer the swings? ____

Show 3:40.

5 + 7 – 8 =

3 nickels and 19 pennies

_____ ¢

Measure the gum to the nearest inch and centimeter.

____ in.

____ cm

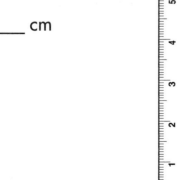
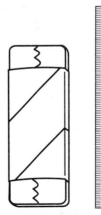

_____ faces

_____ edges

_____ vertices

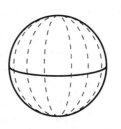

Robert has 35 meters of green twine and 28 meters of brown twine. How many meters of twine does he have in all?

Write **<**, **>**, or **=** to compare.

570 ◯ 670

344 ◯ 343

226 ◯ 216

980 ◯ 975

_____ cm

Use addition to fill in the pyramid. Each number is the sum of the two numbers below it.

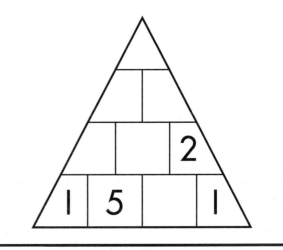

```
  49
+ 32
```

```
  28
  36
+ 45
```

Write the number in words.

**294**

_____

_____

100, 90, _____, _____, _____

Aaron's bakery has 96 bagels. There are 27 blueberry ones. How many of the bagels are not blueberry?

How much longer is one cherry than the other?
_____ cm

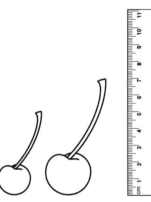

Joss had 57 juice boxes. He shared some with his neighbors. Then he got 24 more juice boxes. Now he has 38 juice boxes. How many did he share?

---

Use the information from the tally chart to complete the line plot.

| Height of Plants | |
|---|---|
| 10 cm | l l l l |
| 11 cm | l l l l l |
| 12 cm | l l l |

Height of Plants

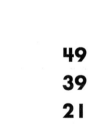

10        11        12

---

**8 hundreds + 7 tens**
**= _____**

---

Divide the rectangle into 4 rows and 5 columns. How many squares are there?

_____

---

49
39
21
+ 19

---

_____ ¢

---

Write the time in words.

9:10

_____

---

14 + 5 − 3 =

13 − 9 + 1 =

28        99        58
+ 64      − 73      − 32
_____     _____     _____

What is the value of the underlined digit?

**37_1_**

◯ 1

◯ 10

◯ 100

Write **<**, **>**, or **=** to compare each pair of numbers.

**212** ◯ **312**

Write a number sentence to match the picture.

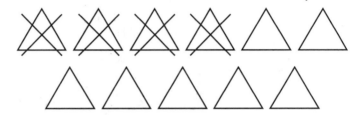

The numbers in the squares are the sums of the numbers in the circles. Write the missing numbers.

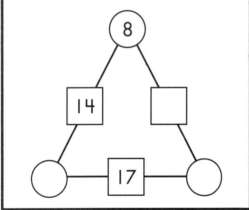

**12 + 9 − 3 =**

Write the number.

two hundred ninety

Debi has one flag that is 50 in. wide and one that is 78 in. wide. How much wider is the bigger flag?

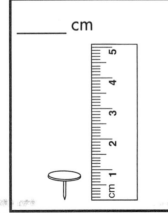
_____ cm

**300 + 80 + 2 =**

**500 + 70 + 4 =**

**100 + 90 + 9 =**

Louis' keyboard has 88 black and white keys. 52 of the keys are white. How many keys are black?

Color four-fourths.

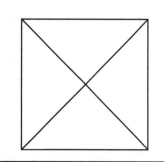

344 + 100 =

Write the missing numbers and circle the operations to get from 53 to 59.

**53**

+ □
− 

**77**

+ □
−

**42**

+ □
−

**59**

Color all of the pentagons.

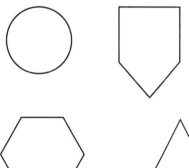

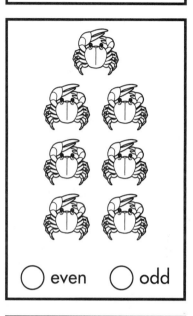

○ even     ○ odd

____ : ____

787 − 10 =

5 nickels, 1 quarter, and 1 penny

_____ ¢

How much taller is one water glass than the other?
_____ cm

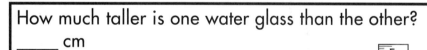

Divide the rectangle into 3 rows and 4 columns. How many squares are there?

_____

Tabitha's back yard is 45 yards long. Her house is 20 yards long. How much longer is her yard than her house?

Complete the fact family.

4 + _____ = 6

2 + 4 = _____

6 - _____ = 2

_____ - 2 = 4

```
  73
- 56
_____
```

Write the number.

4 hundreds, 7 ones

Write the missing numbers.

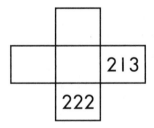

213

222

Measure the seashell to the nearest inch and centimeter.

_____ in.    _____ cm

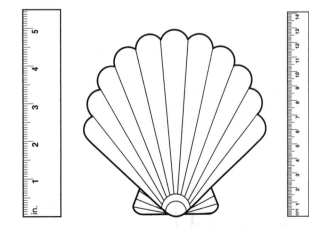

645, 545, _____, _____, _____

Felix has 45 marshmallows and 23 graham crackers. How many more marshmallows than crackers does he have?

Estimate the length of the grasshopper in centimeters. ____ cm

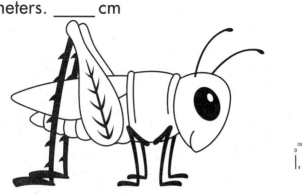

centimeters
0        1

---

Kate had $2 and 45¢. She found a quarter between the couch cushions. How much money does she have now?

---

Kirsten had 25 greeting cards. She wrote cards to some friends and mailed them. Now she has 14 greeting cards. How many cards did she write?

Which number sentence could be used to solve the problem?

○ **25 + 14**

○ **14 – 25**

○ **25 – 14**

○ **14 + 25**

---

$18 - 4 - 10 + 9 =$

---

Color one third of each rectangle.

---

____ cm

---

Show the number sentence on the number line.

**28 – 16**

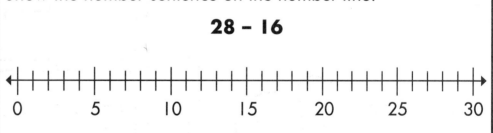

0        5        10        15        20        25        30

---

| 328 | | |
|---|---|---|
| Hundreds | Tens | Ones |
| | | |

---

Write **<**, **>**, or **=** to compare.

**241** ○ **441**

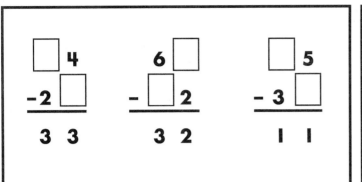

□4
−2□
**3 3**

6□
−□2
**3 2**

□5
−3□
**1 1**

Seth drove his truck 26 miles. Then he drove another 67 miles. How many miles did he drive in all?

Circle the greater number.

600 + 70 + 6

600 + 80

Add to find the missing numbers.

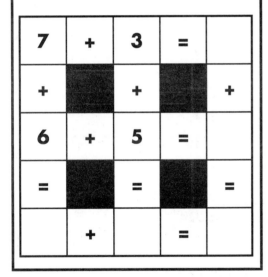

| 7 | + | 3 | = | |
|---|---|---|---|---|
| + | | + | | + |
| 6 | + | 5 | = | |
| = | | = | | = |
| | + | | = | |

How many more people prefer mint than cinnamon?

_____

How many people prefer bubblegum flavor? _____

How many more people prefer bubblegum than cinnamon? _____

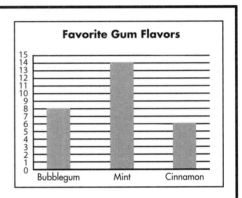

**Favorite Gum Flavors**

Bubblegum     Mint     Cinnamon

**405 + 10 =**

Write the number.

eight hundred twenty

Mischa had 38 crickets. Her pet lizard ate some crickets, so she bought 24 more. Now she has 40 crickets. How many did the lizard eat?

____ + 3 = 6

4 + ____ = 8

5 + 5 = ____

25
+ 45
____

70
− 35
____

Ebony had 30 hairclips. Her mother gave her some more. Then, she had 55. How many did her mother give her?

Draw a shape with 5 angles.

**102 ◯ 201**

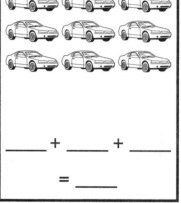

_____ + _____ + _____

= _____

_____ in.

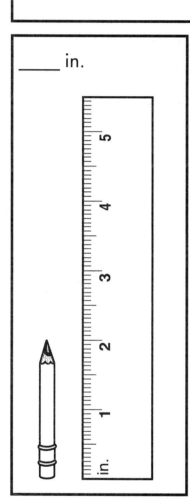

Make a drawing that includes rectangles, squares, trapezoids, triangles, half-circles, and quarter-circles.

$$\begin{array}{r} 28 \\ 33 \\ 15 \\ +\ 91 \\ \hline \end{array}$$

9 + 9 =

800 + 60 =

Who has more money?

Jocelyn's money:

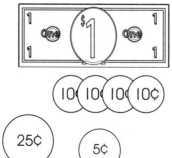

Rodney's money:

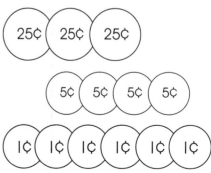

The distance from your nose to your toes is about:

○ 3 feet          ○ 3 in.

○ 3 meters     ○ 3 cm

Label the parts.
Color two-thirds.

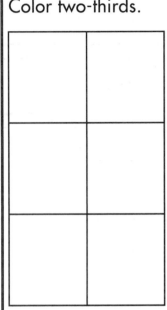

_____ : _____

Which is longer? _____

How much longer? _____

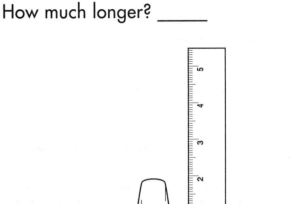

66
− 39

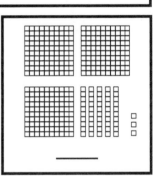

_____

Last year Kathryn's hair was 5 in. long. Now it has grown 6 more in. If she wants to cut it to be only 4 in. long, how many in. should she cut?

567 + 100 = _____

Count by tens. How many golf balls?

_____

○ 16 − 2 = 13
○ 14 + 1 = 16
○ 16 − 3 = 11
○ 15 + 2 = 17

Match each item to the unit you would use to measure it.

**height of an ant**                    **feet**

**height of a door**                    **cm**

**length of a trip to the store**        **miles**

Draw a rectangle that is made of 6 square units.

```
.   .   .   .   .

.   .   .   .   .

.   .   .   .   .

.   .   .   .   .

.   .   .   .   .
```

Draw a bar graph to show the following: In Jessie's class, 5 children have cats, 3 children have dogs, 2 children have hamsters and 1 child has a guinea pig.

**90 − 50 =**

Write the missing numbers.

| 75 |    | 77 |
|----|----|----|
|    | 86 |    |
|    |    |    |

31
54
48
+ 29

Jayden had 8 super hero figurines. He gave 5 to his friend. Then his brother gave him 7 more. How many does Jayden have now? Use the number line to solve the problem.

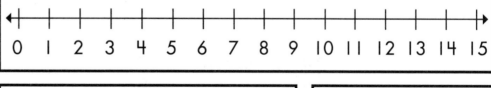

0  1  2  3  4  5  6  7  8  9  10  11  12  13  14  15

**209**

| Hundreds | Tens | Ones |
|----------|------|------|
|          |      |      |

Write **<**, **>**, or **=** to compare.

**521 ◯ 384**

| 62 | 98 | 74 |
|---|---|---|
| − 51 | − 38 | − 27 |

Jamie read 18 pages on Monday, 16 pages on Tuesday, and 29 pages on Wednesday. How many pages did Jamie read so far this week?

Which is true?

◯ A square has six sides.

◯ A cube has six faces.

Color an even number of bananas.

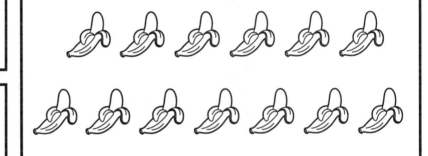

Cross out the base ten blocks to solve the problem.

**545 − 215 = ____**

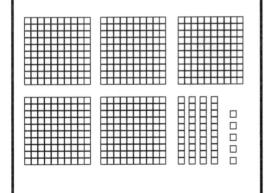

**787 − 200 =**

Draw four different quadrilaterals.

Write the number.

nine hundred twenty one

5

◯

+ _____

13

Write the numbers in expanded form.

**53 = _____**

**305 = _____**

Juanita got eighty-five cents in allowance last week. She will get one hundred thirty-five cents this week. How much will she have all together?

Color four-fourths.

16 + 19 =

○ even    ○ odd

Count by 5s up the ladder

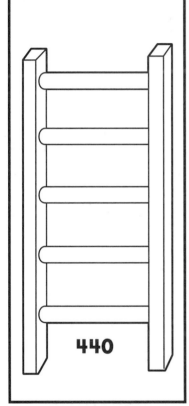

440

68 – 44 =

529

____ hundreds

____ tens

____ ones

Number of Laps Students Ran

```
        x       x
        x       x
        x               x
  x     x       x       x
  x     x       x       x
```

| 2 | 3 | 4 | 5 |

How many children ran 4 laps?

_____

How many more children ran 5 laps than 2 laps? _____

How many laps did the greatest number of children run? _____

Show 1:30.

Write **<**, **>**, or **=** to compare.

298 ◯ 398          105 ◯ 501

888 ◯ 777          920 ◯ 392

485 ◯ 486          715 ◯ 751

I have 5 sides. What am I?

○ cube

○ hexagon

○ pentagon

Draw an array to match the number sentence.

**2 + 2 + 2 + 2 = 8**

Write **<**, **>**, or **=** to compare.

235 ○ 325

683 ○ 386

503 ○ 239

125 ○ 910

Cross out the base ten blocks to solve the problem.

**585 − 233 = _____**

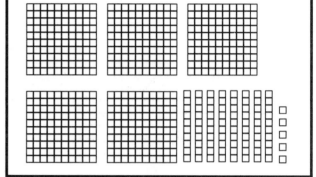

```
  325
+ 181
```

```
  33
  41
+ 58
```

Write the number in words.

**821**

_____

_____

**521 − 100 = ____**

Sam has 32 raisins and 18 bananas. How many pieces of fruit does he have?

**+4**

0

7

1

4

3

9

Estimate the length of the rectangle. _____ in.

Inches

0                    1

Which number sentence could you use to solve the problem?

**? – 24 = 51**

◯ 51 – 24

◯ 51 + 24

◯ 24 – 51

◯ 24 + 34

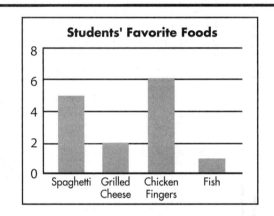

How many students like spaghetti best? _____

How many more students like chicken fingers than fish? _____

How many students like grilled cheese? _____

**876 = _____ hundreds + _____ tens + _____ ones**

Draw an array to match the number sentence.

**3 + 3 + 3 = 9**

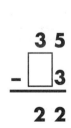

```
  3 5
-   3
─────
  2 2
```

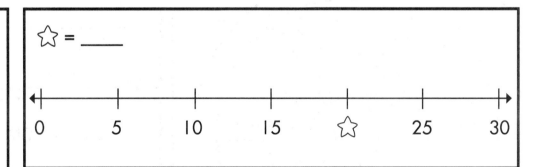

☆ = _____

Jamal has 3 dimes and 2 quarters in his pocket. How much does Jamal have?

Write **<**, **>**, or **=** to compare.

**239 ◯ 225**

Elizabeth bought 23 glittery stickers and 39 bows. She used 20 of the decorations on presents. How many does she have left?

What is the value of the 2 in each number?

**328** ____        **290** ____

**152** ____        **102** ____

Circle the greater number.

three hundred seventy

three hundred seven

Color an even number of trucks.

Solve each problem. Draw an **X** on problems with an even sum. Draw an **O** on problems with an odd sum.

| 3 + 6 | 12 + 6 | 16 – 3 |
|-------|--------|--------|
| 14 – 9 | 17+2 | 11 – 4 |
| 13 – 2 | 6+10 | 4 + 8 |

**97 + 25 + 21 =**

Write the number in words.

**35**

_____

The grocery store has 18 zucchinis and 46 eggplants. How many items of produce are in the section?

Write the doubles fact.

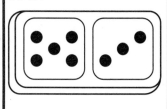

____ + ____ = ____

**200 + 60 =**

**200 + 10 + 6 =**

**200 + 6 =**

Freddy ran 15 laps yesterday, and he ran more today. All together Freddy ran 29 laps. How many laps did Freddy run today?

Draw a shape that has 6 sides.

**339** ◯ **993**

_____ + _____ + _____

= _____

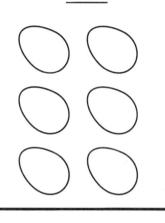

_____ cm

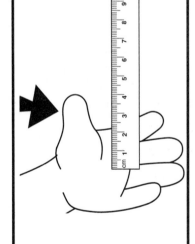

Draw and name a closed three-sided shape.

_____

```
  79
  19
  50
+ 31
```

**5 + 15 =**

**500 − 30 =**

In which week did Sophie earn the most allowance?

Sophie's allowance last week:

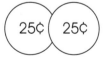

Sophie's allowance this week:

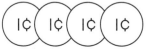

Divide the rectangle into 4 equal parts.

Add to find the missing numbers. Each number is the sum of the two numbers below it.

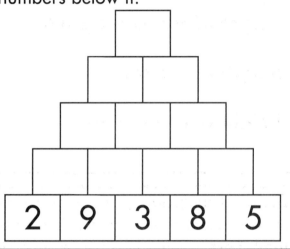

| 2 | 9 | 3 | 8 | 5 |

Write a number sentence for the array.

Write **<**, **>**, or **=** to compare.

226 ◯ 262

342 ◯ 352

591 ◯ 592

878 ◯ 878

289
− 95

**287**

_____ hundreds

_____ tens

_____ ones

9 + 5 − 3 =

15 + 4 − 3 =

19 − 8 + 4 =

532 + 10 = _____

_____ in.

5

4

3

2

1

in.

Ricky saw 15 animals in his backyard today. Elhaj saw 49 animals in his backyard. How many more animals did Elhaj see today?

Match each item to the unit you would use to measure it.

**height of a second grader**          feet

**length of a banana**                meters

**height of a building**                inches

---

Draw a rectangle that is made of 12 square units.

. . . . .

. . . . .

. . . . .

. . . . .

. . . . .

---

Draw a bar graph to show the following: Six of Maria's classmates like reading best, five like math best, seven like science best, and three like gym best.

---

**30 + 20 =**

---

Write the missing numbers.

|    | 24 |    |
|----|----|----|
| 33 |    |    |
|    |    | 45 |

---

```
  31
  54
  48
+ 29
```

---

Shana had 9 pencils. Then she gave her younger sister 2. How many does she have now?

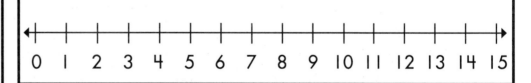

0  1  2  3  4  5  6  7  8  9  10  11  12  13  14  15

---

Write the time in words.

_____

---

Write **<**, **>**, or **=** to compare.

**198 ◯ 809**

102          330          801
+ 521        + 101        + 125

Write the value of the underlined digit.

20**6** ____          98**3** ____

**4**45 ____          2**3**5 ____

How many faces? _____

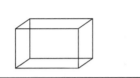

Add to find the missing numbers. Each number is the sum of the two numbers below it.

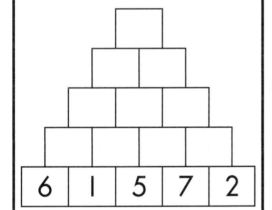

| 6 | 1 | 5 | 7 | 2 |

○ even     ○ odd

18 − 10 =

Divide the rectangle into thirds.

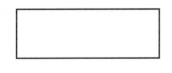

Jenny's kitchen is 35 feet long and her bedroom is 26 feet long. How much longer is her kitchen than her bedroom?

Choose the best estimate for the length of a tiger.

○ 10 feet

○ 10 inches

○ 10 meters

Write the numbers in expanded form.

**238** = _____

**301** = _____

Arthur baked 24 muffins, 24 cupcakes, and 36 cookies. How many items did he bake?

Color one-third.

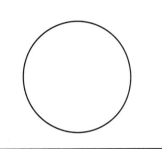

8 + 9 =

222 + 100 =

539 + 100 =

Skip count by 100 up the ladder.

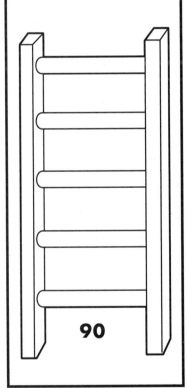

90

Draw a picture that uses at least one shape that has three sides, two different shapes that have four angles, and one shape that has five sides.

**532**

_____ hundreds

_____ tens

_____ ones

13 + 6 =

Show 10:25.

Draw 2 ways to make 38¢.

Ruby has 56 place mats and 29 napkins for her restaurant. How many more place mats than napkins does she have?

Solve each problem. Draw an **X** on a problem with an even sum and an **O** on a problem with an odd sum.

| 3 + 9 | 14 + 6 | 19 − 3 |
|-------|--------|--------|
| 19 − 9 | 12 + 2 | 15 − 4 |
| 17 − 2 | 9 + 10 | 4 + 7 |

Divide the circle into fourths. Color and label one-fourth.

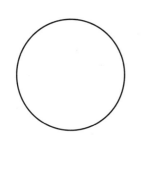

___ : ___

$$\begin{array}{r} 91 \\ -\ 39 \\ \hline \end{array}$$

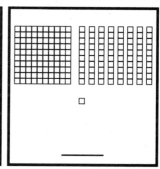

_____

Last year Allen could jump 12 in. Now he can jump 18 in. If he wants to jump 24 in., how much more does he have to be able to jump?

Count by 5s. How many lizards? _____

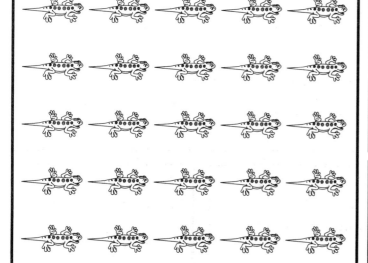

195, 190, _____, _____, _____

Which number sentence is true?

◯ 17 − 2 = 13      ◯ 13 − 3 = 11

◯ 19 − 5 = 16      ◯ 6 + 12 = 18

Estimate the height of the cube.

_____ cm

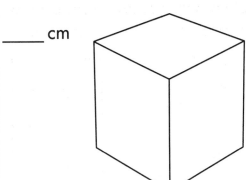

centimeters
0    1

---

**? − 19 = 81**
Which number sentence would be best for solving the problem?

○ 81 − 19
○ 81 + 19
○ 19 + 81
○ 19 − 81

---

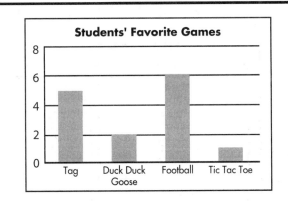

**Students' Favorite Games**

How many students like tic-tac-toe best? _____

How many more students like football than tag?

_____

How many students like duck duck goose? _____

---

**35 =**
_____ **tens +** _____ **ones**

---

Draw an array to match the number sentence.

**4 + 4 + 4 = 12**

---

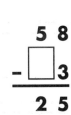

```
  5 8
-  □ 3
 ─────
  2 5
```

---

☆ = _____

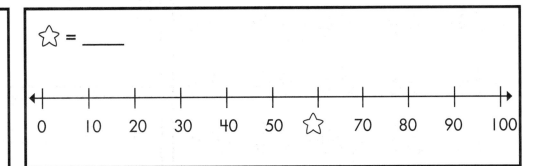

0   10   20   30   40   50   ☆   70   80   90   100

---

Lee's dad gave him 3 quarters and 3 nickels for cleaning the bathroom. How much did Lee make?

---

Write **<**, **>**, or **=** to compare.

**533** ○ **533**

$$62 + 51$$    $$98 + 38$$    $$74 + 27$$

Serene built a castle with 34 blocks on Tuesday. She used 29 blocks on Wednesday. She used 19 blocks on Thursday. How many blocks did she use in all?

Draw a shape that has four angles.

$19 +$ △ $= 34$      $52 -$ ◯ $= 27$

△ $=$ ____      ◯ $=$ ____

The numbers below are scrambled. Put them in order by drawing a line to connect them. The line has been started for you.

| 10 | 5 | 75 |
| --- | --- | --- |
| 15 | 65 | 70 |
| 50 | 20 | 60 |
| 45 | 55 | 25 |
| 40 | 35 | 30 |

$$97 + 25 + 21 =$$

Write the number.

four hundred thirty five

The bakery has 24 muffins and 18 bagels. How many baked goods do they have?

Draw dots to complete the doubles fact.

$$3 + 3 = 6$$

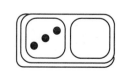

$$400 + 20 =$$

$$400 + 30 + 2 =$$

$$300 + 40 + 3 =$$

The ice rink has 50 pairs of skates. They have 32 pairs left. How many people have a pair of rented skates?

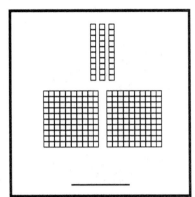

_____

**16 − 8 =**

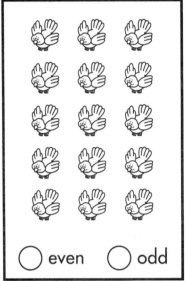

◯ even   ◯ odd

Draw base ten blocks to match the number.
**322**

| Number of Shooting Stars Seen | |
|---|---|
| Monday | ✸ ✸ ✸ ✸ ✸ ✸ |
| Wednesday | ✸ ✸ ✸ ✸ |
| Friday | ✸ ✸ ✸ |

How many stars did they see all together? _____

How many more stars did they see on Wednesday than on Friday? _____

_____ : _____

**12 + 3 =**

7 dimes and 1 quarter

_____ ¢

| Number Words | Hundreds _____ |
|---|---|
| | Tens _____ |
| | Ones _____ |
| Expanded Form | Base Ten Blocks |

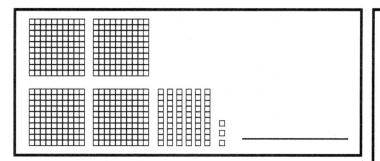 _____

Sam has washed 39 knives, 28 spoons, and 19 forks. How many pieces of silverware did Sam wash?

Write the fact family for the numbers.

**12    3    9**

___ + ___ = ___

___ + ___ = ___

___ – ___ = ___

___ – ___ = ___

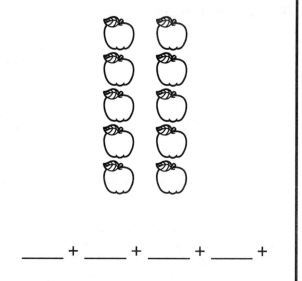

___ + ___ + ___ + ___ +

___ = ___

| | |
|---|---|
| 566<br>– 277 | 87<br>12<br>+ 29 |

Write the number in words.

**239**

_____

_____

Use the number line to solve the problem.

**80 – 50 = ___**

```
0  10  20  30  40  50  60  70  80  90  100
```

330, _____, 310, _____, _____

Jamie has 93 crackers and 39 pieces of cheese. How many sandwiches can Jamie make if each one requires 2 crackers and 1 piece of cheese?

Match the numbers.

235                          805

eight hundred five          200 + 30 + 5

eight hundred fifteen       800 + 10 + 5

---

Draw a rectangle that is made of 10 equal parts.

```
.   .   .   .   .   .
.   .   .   .   .   .
.   .   .   .   .   .
.   .   .   .   .   .
.   .   .   .   .   .
```

---

Draw a tally chart to show the following: In Jessie's class, 3 children have no siblings, 4 children have a sister, 5 children have a brother and 2 children have a sister and a brother.

---

260 – 100 =

Write a number sentence to match the array.

---

89
24
38
+ 19

---

Alexandra made 8 muffins. Then, she and her mother and sister each ate one. How many muffins did she have left? Draw on the number line to solve the problem.

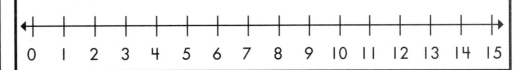

0  1  2  3  4  5  6  7  8  9  10  11  12  13  14  15

---

| 473 | | |
|-----|-----|-----|
| Hundreds | Tens | Ones |
| | | |

---

Write <, >, or = to compare.

299 ◯ 901

$$\begin{array}{r} 231 \\ + 521 \\ \hline \end{array} \qquad \begin{array}{r} 330 \\ - 101 \\ \hline \end{array} \qquad \begin{array}{r} 901 \\ - 225 \\ \hline \end{array}$$

Write the values of the underlined digits.

1̲03 _____          82̲1 _____

2̲29 _____          2̲35 _____

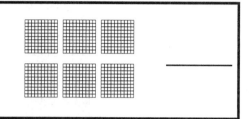 _____

Write a doubles fact for each domino.

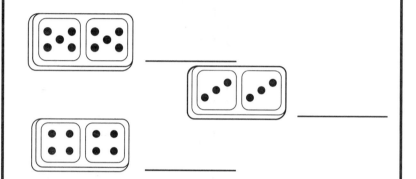

_____

_____

_____

Add to find the missing numbers. Each number is the sum of the two numbers below it.

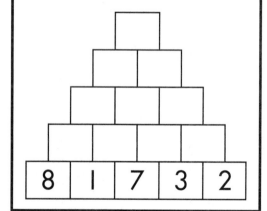

| 8 | 1 | 7 | 3 | 2 |

39 – 11 =

Divide the circle into fourths.

Mike has 39 feet of fishing line. Julian has 15 feet. How much more fishing line does Mike have?

Choose the best estimate for the height of a tall tree.

○ 4 yards
○ 4 in.
○ 4 feet
○ 4 cm

Write the numbers in expanded form.

**911 =** _____

**313 =** _____

There were 78 people at the class play. Some fire fighters left to deal with an alarm. Sixteen people came late. At the end, there were 90 people. How many fire fighters left?

How much is shaded? _____

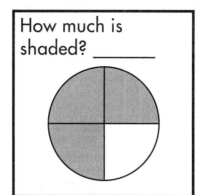

**170 + 10 =**

Estimate the length of the grasshopper in centimeters.

_____ cm

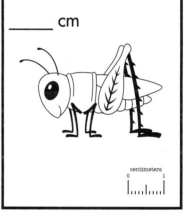

centimeters
0          1

Count by 100s to fill in the missing ladder rungs.

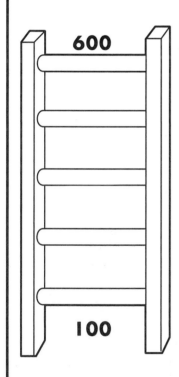

**600**

**100**

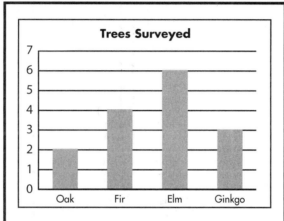

**Trees Surveyed**

Mr. Harris's class did a tree survey.

Did the class see more elm trees or fir trees? _____

How many more ginkgo trees did they see than oak? _____

Show 4:55.

**600 − 200 =**

6 quarters and 12 nickels

_____ ¢

Measure the centipede to the nearest inch and centimeter.

_____ in.

_____ cm

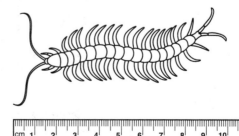

Finish partitioning the rectangle.

Draw an array to match the number sentence.

**3 + 3 + 3 + 3 = 12**

Joshua had 92¢. He gave his little brother a dime and a nickel. How much does Joshua have left?

Which number sentence does not belong in the fact family?

○ 4 + 11 = 15

○ 15 − 4 = 11

○ 11 + 4 = 15

○ 11 − 15 = 4

$$\begin{array}{r} 62 \\ -\ 57 \\ \hline \end{array}$$

$$\begin{array}{r} 36 \\ 32 \\ +\ 18 \\ \hline \end{array}$$

Write the number in words.

**800**

_____

785, 780, _____, _____, _____

____ : ____

**16 + 12 + 6 − 7 =**

**19 − 13 + 6 − 2 =**

Estimate the length of the rectangle.
_____ cm

centimeters
0        1

---

**? – 34 = 84**
Which number sentence would be best for solving the problem?

○ 84 – 34
○ 84 + 34
○ 34 – 84
○ 34 + 34

---

| School Trip Choices | |
|---|---|
| Museum | ☆ ☆ |
| Circus | ☆ ☆ ☆ ☆ ☆ ☆ |
| Forest | ☆ ☆ ☆ |
| Beach | ☆ ☆ ☆ ☆ |

☆ = 1 person

How many people want to go to the beach? _____
How many more people prefer the circus to the forest? _____
How many people want to go to the museum?
_____

---

**16 – 3 – 10 =**

---

Divide the rectangles into fourths two different ways.

---

8 3
– 4 ☐
—————
4 1

---

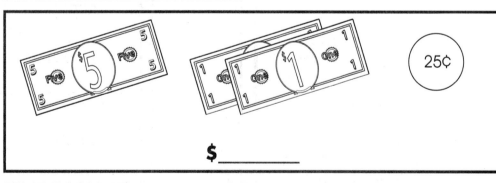

$ _____

---

Write the time in words.

6:35

_____

---

Write **<**, **>**, or **=** to compare.

**257 ◯ 256**

---

☐6          2 1          5 9
+2 3        +7☐          +☐5
─────       ─────        ─────
  8 9         9 9          9 4

Write the value of the 8 in each number.

832 ____          118 ____

208 ____          181 ____

Write <, >, or = to compare.

897 ◯ 986

Color an even number of lollipops.

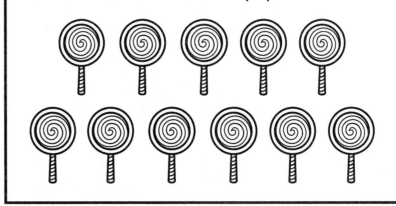

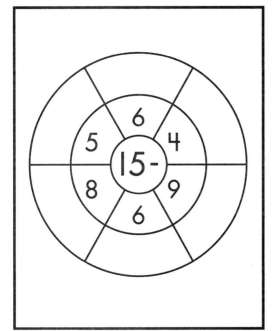

70 – 30 =

Write the number.

four hundred sixteen

Bruce bought an apple for 78¢. He gave the cashier a five-dollar bill. How much change did he get?

A dog would most likely be _____ tall.

◯ 15 in.

◯ 15 cm

◯ 15 yards

68          76
- 33        - 72
────        ────

Tanya baked 55 loaves of bread. She sold some. Then she baked 25 more. Now Tanya has 27 loaves of bread. How many did she sell?

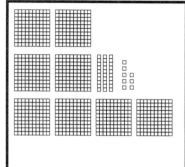

_____

$11 - 7 =$

Color an even number of cars.

Write the missing numbers and circle the operations to get from 88 to 25.

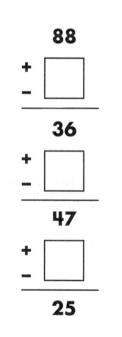

**88**

+ [ ]
−

**36**

+ [ ]
−

**47**

+ [ ]
−

**25**

Favorite Animal at the Zoo

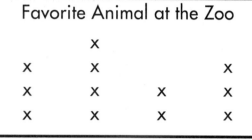

**Tigers    Monkeys   Penguins    Seals**

How many students liked tigers best? ____

Which animal was picked by the most students? _____

Were seals or monkeys more popular? _____

Show 5:05.

$339 + 20 =$

2 quarters, 3 nickels, 2 dimes, 1 penny

_____ ¢

| Number Words | Hundreds ____ |
| --- | --- |
| | Tens ____ |
| | Ones ____ |
| Expanded Form | Base Ten Blocks |

Divide the rectangle into thirds.

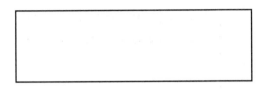

Draw an array to match the number sentence.

**2 + 2 + 2 + 2 = 8**

Write the fact family for the numbers.

**6    5    11**

___ + ___ = ___

___ + ___ = ___

___ − ___ = ___

___ − ___ = ___

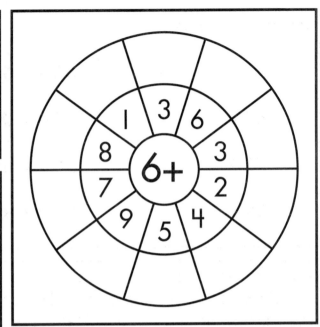

| 236 |
| + 122 |

| 82 |
| 35 |
| + 35 |

Write the number in words:

**450**

_____

_____

450, 440, _____, _____, _____

**Items Sold at the Second Grade Bake Sale**

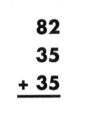

How many brownies were sold? _____

How many more cookies were sold than pies? _____

What item was sold the least? _____

Bob counted 18 birds and 38 bugs. How many creatures did he count in all?

Match the numbers.

502          500 + 20

512          500 + 2

520          500 + 20 + 1

521          500 + 10 + 2

---

Eddie had 72¢. Then, he found a quarter, a dime, and 2 nickels. How much money does he have now?

---

Lila's father bought 85 peas and 45 baby tomatoes at the farmers market. He used 48 of the vegetables in a recipe. What operation do you need to use to find out how many vegetables he has left?

○ addition only

○ addition and subtraction

○ subtraction only

---

397 = ___ **hundreds** + ___ **tens** + ___ **ones**

---

Draw a rectangle that can be divided into 18 equal parts.

. . . . . . . .

. . . . . . . .

. . . . . . . .

. . . . . . . .

. . . . . . . .

---

41
9
42
+ 8

---

Which number sentence does the number line show?

○ **30 – 20**      ○ **30 – 10**      ○ **20 + 30**

0   5   10   15   20   25   30   35   40   45   50

---

Write the time in words.

_____

---

Write **<**, **>**, or **=** to compare.

**251 ○ 215**

---

John picked 59 blueberries. His brother gave him some more. Then, Jacob ate 33 blueberries. Now, he has 40. How many blueberries did John get from his brother?

Write the value of the underlined digit in each number.

**33<u>6</u>** ___          **6<u>3</u>3** ___

**6<u>6</u>3** ___          **<u>3</u>66** ___

Circle the greater number.

400 + 80 + 7

400 + 70

Color an even number of boxes

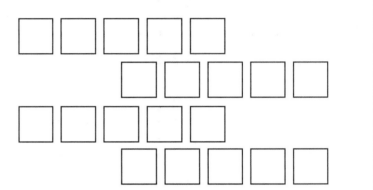

Cross out base ten blocks to subtract.

**382 – 101 = ___**

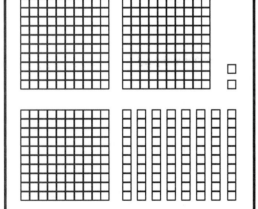

**388 – 10 =**

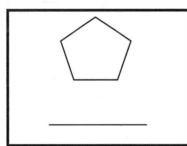

_____

Dre had a dollar, 4 nickels and six pennies. Then, 6 found 1 quarter. How much money does he have now?

Write the doubles fact.

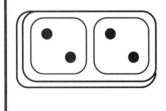

___ + ___ = ___

277
+ 289

691
+ 208

Denita made 16 bracelets, 22 brooches, and 19 necklaces. How many pieces of jewelry did she make?

Color two-thirds.

8 + 9 =

534 – 100 =

Skip count by 100 up the ladder.

90

Draw a picture that uses at least 2 shapes with three angles and 1 shape with six angles.

982

____ hundreds

____ tens

____ ones

11 + 8 =

Draw 2 ways to make 56¢.

Show 10:25.

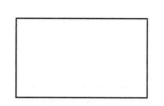

Draw a cylinder.

---

Draw a line through three facts in the grid that have the same sum.

| 13 + 9 | 14 + 6 | 19 − 3 |
|--------|--------|--------|
| 15 − 7 | 12 + 10 | 15 − 4 |
| 18 − 2 | 9 + 10 | 11 + 11 |

---

Amie had $34. She spent $29 on groceries. How much money does she have left?

---

Write **<**, **>**, or **=** to compare.

**326** ◯ **426**

**199** ◯ **200**

**712** ◯ **721**

**713** ◯ **713**

---

$$\begin{array}{r} 65 \\ -\ 29 \\ \hline \end{array}$$

$$\begin{array}{r} 56 \\ 34 \\ +\ 72 \\ \hline \end{array}$$

---

Color the shape that has an odd number of sides.

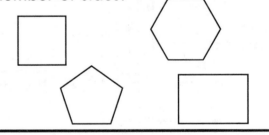

---

**Favorite Desserts**

| | 7 | 6 | 5 | 4 | 3 | 2 | 1 | 0 |

(bar graph: Cake = 3, Ice Cream = 5, Pie = 6, Brownies = 3)

Which dessert do the most people like?

_____

How many people like ice cream? _____

How many more people like pie than brownies? _____

---

140, 150, _____, _____, _____

---

Which number sentence is true?

◯ 7 − 8 = 15      ◯ 9 − 3 = 112

◯ 6 + 5 = 12      ◯ 8 + 9 = 17

Name _____

Match each shape to its name.

**cube**

**square**

**rectangular prism**

---

Ahmed has 36 erasers. Ashley has 19 erasers. How many more erasers does Ahmed have?

---

Mac's cookie recipe calls for 50 walnuts and 38 almonds. She has 48 nuts. What operation do you need to use to find out how many nuts she is missing?

○ Add, then subtract.

○ Add, then add again.

○ Subtract, then add.

○ Subtract, then subtract again.

---

$5 + 6 - 8 =$

---

Draw a three-dimensional figure with six faces.

---

```
 11
 62
+21
```

---

Use the number line to solve the problem.

$$20 + 50 = \_\_\_$$

0  10  20  30  40  50  60  70  80  90  100

---

Write the time in words.

_____

---

Write **<**, **>**, or **=** to compare.

517 ○ 561

---

Bob's Restaurant has 61 dishes on the menu. Jane's Restaurant has 22 dishes that it serves. How many more dishes are available at Bob's Restaurant?

---

Write the value of the 5 in each number.

**656** ____    **599** ____

**305** ____    **150** ____

---

How many sides does an octagon have?

○ 5    ○ 8    ○ 6

---

Draw a line through the squares whose facts have the same answers.

| | | |
|---|---|---|
| 13 − 9 | 14 − 6 | 19 + 3 |
| 15 − 7 | 12 − 8 | 15 − 4 |
| 18 − 4 | 9 + 5 | 11 − 7 |

---

+

_____ animals

---

**30 + 100 =**

---

Write the number.

three hundred twenty-eight

---

Ms. Singh's class has 11 girls and 14 boys, Mr. Espino's class has 23 children. How many fewer children are in Mr. Espino's class?

---

____ in.

---

**800 + 30 + 2 = ____**

**70 + 5 = ____**

**300 + 20 = ____**

Milli has 32 books. Emmett has 26 books. How many more books does Milli have?

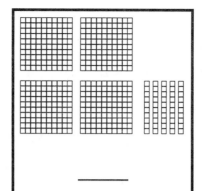

_____

$15 + 5 =$

Draw two different shapes with four sides.

Draw base ten blocks to match the number.
**106**

| Animals Seen at the Farm | |
|---|---|
| Allen | |
| Shamiah | |
| Britney | |
| Juan | = 1 animal |

Which child saw the fewest animals? _____

Who saw more animals Shamiah or Britney? _____

Which students saw the same number of animals? _____
_____

Write the number.

4 hundreds, 3 tens, 9 ones

$730 - 100 =$

Draw and label two ways to make 40¢.

six thirty-five

Joshua buys 26 bibs, and his wife separately buys some too. If Joshua then uses 6 bibs on the baby, and they have 44, how many bibs did Joshua's wife buy?

Draw an array to match the number sentence.

**3 + 3 + 3 + 3 + 3 = 15**

Write the fact family for the numbers.

**12      5      17**

___ + ___ = ___

___ + ___ = ___

___ - ___ = ___

___ - ___ = ___

6+

1 3 6
8        3
7        2
9 5 4

**36**
**+ 37**
_____

**344**

_____ hundreds

_____ tens

_____ ones

Lisa painted a mural that was 36 feet long this summer. Last summer she painted a mural that was 8 feet long. How much longer is her mural this summer?

_____ feet

Chris and Martin cut pieces of string and then measured them. Use the line plot to answer the questions.

```
                      x
           x          x          x
x          x          x          x
x          x          x          x
_____
55 cm      60 cm      65 cm      70 cm
```

How long was the longest string? _____

Which length had the most string? _____

330, 340, _____, _____, _____

Farmer Jones has 23 apple trees and 96 cherry trees. How many more cherry trees does Farmer Jones have?

Draw a beach scene with 2 quadrilaterals, 1 pentagon, and 2 triangles.

Tomas picked 94 strawberries. He gave some to his sister for a pie, and then he picked 35 more. Now he has 64 strawberries. How many did he give away?

| Family Reunion Food Options | |
|---|---|
| Pizza |  |
| Chicken | ⬯ |
| Burgers | ⬯ ⬯ ⬯ ⬯ |
| Tacos | ⬯ ⬯ |

⬯ = 1 meal

How many more family members ate tacos than chicken? ____

How many people ate the two most popular options together? ____

How many people ate a meal at the family reunion? ____

**260 =**
**___ hundreds + ___ tens**

Draw a rectangle that can be divided into 10 square units.

. . . . . .

. . . . . .

. . . . . .

. . . . . .

. . . . . .

. . . . . .

$$\begin{array}{r} 5\ 3 \\ -\ \square\ 1 \\ \hline 4\ 2 \end{array}$$

Which ones name or show three-dimensional shapes?

○ square   ○ sphere   ○ rectangle   ○ rectangular prism

Tamika grew 39 plants. Then, she planted some more. Now she has 50. How many did Tamika add?

19 – 7 =

17 – 8 =

|        |        |        |
|--------|--------|--------|
| 83     | 64     | 92     |
| − 51   | − 35   | − 27   |

What is the value of the underlined number?

**3_45**

○ four ones

○ four tens

○ four hundreds

Circle the greater number.

$600 + 60 + 3$

$600 + 50 + 9$

**Number of Uncles Kids Have**

| 1 Uncle  | 🚶 🚶         |
|----------|---------------|
| 2 Uncles | 🚶 🚶 🚶 🚶   |
| 3 Uncles | 🚶 🚶 🚶      |
| 4 Uncles | 🚶 🚶 🚶      |

🚶 = 1 uncle

What is the most common number of uncles? _____ Least common? _____

Circle each pair of numbers that adds to 10. Some pairs are side by side, and others are up and down.

| 1  | 9  | 4  | 10 | 1  | 12 |
|----|----|----|----|----|----|
| 7  | 2  | 8  | 0  | 6  | 4  |
| 4  | 11 | 3  | 7  | 3  | 6  |
| 12 | 5  | 6  | 8  | 6  | 9  |
| 8  | 5  | 9  | 1  | 3  | 7  |
| 8  | 2  | 10 | 0  | 11 | 2  |

**789 − 100 =**

Write the number.

seven hundred
thirty-two

Alison has 17 fiction books and 42 nonfiction books on her bookshelf. Barbara has 36 fiction books on her bookshelf. How many more books are on Alison's bookshelf?

Which measurement is longer?

○ 1 foot

○ 1 meter

**46 + 31 =**

○ 75        ○ 15

○ 77        ○ 17

Ms. Pendleton bought 75 grapes. She gave 56 to her students. How many are left?

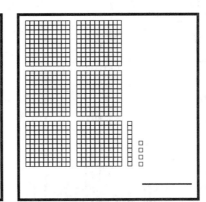

_____

**9 + 7 =**

Color an odd number of stars.

Color 268.

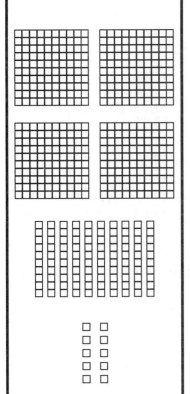

Draw 4 different triangles by adding to the lines provided.

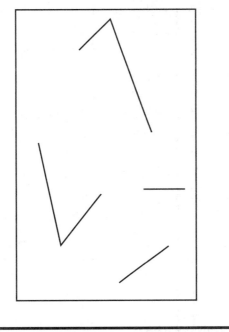

Show 11:20.

**200 + 10 =**

1 quarter 2 dimes, 3 nickels

_____ ¢

____ in.

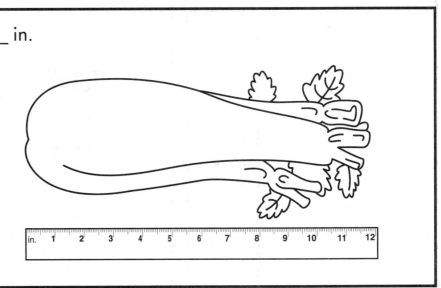

Divide the rectangle into 6 equal parts.

_____ + _____ = _____

Paul had 59 minerals in his collection. He found 13 new minerals over the weekend. How many minerals does he have now?

Write **<**, **>**, or **=** to compare.

650 ◯ 550

321 ◯ 320

573 ◯ 853

418 ◯ 417

347
+ 287

23
12
+ 41

Write the number in words.

**292**

_____

_____

Which of the following would be a good choice to measure your height?

◯ meterstick          ◯ inch ruler

◯ centimeter ruler    ◯ scale

998 − 100 =

11 + 7 =

_____ in.

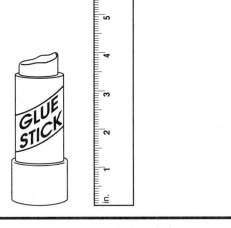

Divide the rectangle into thirds.

Paula had 82 stickers. She made cards with 23 stickers and then bought some more stickers. Now she has 90 stickers. What operation do you need to use to find out how many stickers she bought?

- ○ Add, then add again.
- ○ Add, then subtract.
- ○ Subtract, then subtract again.
- ○ Subtract, then add.

$16 - 9 + 4 =$

Color the quadrilateral.

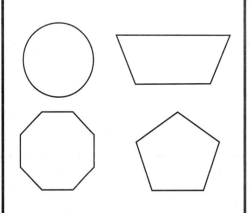

$$\begin{array}{r} \boxed{\phantom{0}}6 \\ +\ 4\ 6 \\ \hline 9\ 2 \end{array}$$

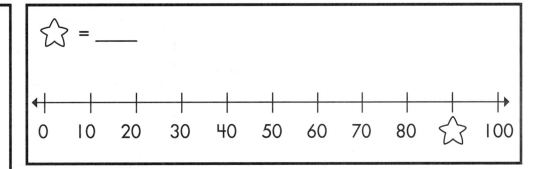

☆ = _____

Alfredo has 24 big leaves and 35 small leaves in his leaf collection. How many leaves does he have?

Write **<**, **>**, or **=** to compare.

$$416 \bigcirc 461$$

```
   2 1          4 ☐          2 1
 + ☐ 3        + 3 2        + 5 ☐
 ─────        ─────        ─────
   8 4          7 6          7 9
```

Samantha has 45 feet of rope. She needs 65 feet. How many more feet of rope does she need?

$8 + 9 - 10 =$

Color an odd number of turtles.

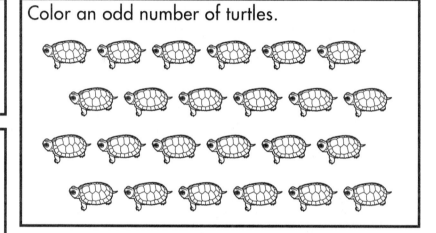

Circle each pair of numbers that equals 15. Some pairs are side by side, and others are up and down.

| 6 | 9 | 4 | 10 | 5 | 12 |
|----|----|----|----|----|----|
| 7 | 2 | 8 | 5 | 6 | 3 |
| 4 | 11 | 3 | 7 | 8 | 6 |
| 12 | 13 | 6 | 8 | 6 | 9 |
| 3 | 2 | 9 | 1 | 3 | 0 |
| 8 | 7 | 14 | 1 | 11 | 15 |

$14 + 10 =$

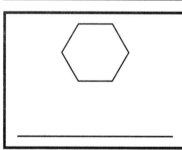

_____

How tall is the glue stick?

_____ cm

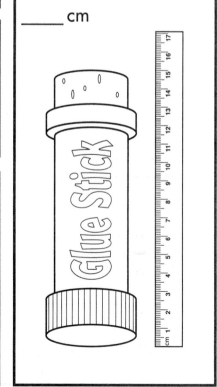

Draw an array to solve the problem.

$4 + 4 + 4 =$ ____

```
  555          398
+ 223        - 277
─────        ─────
```

Ms. Jacinski had 52 pieces of construction paper. Her class used 38 of them in an art project. How many does she have left?

| 6 | + | 7 | = | |
|---|---|---|---|---|
| + | ■ | + | ■ | + |
| 4 | + | 2 | = | |
| = | ■ | = | ■ | = |
| | + | | = | |

19 – 12 =

Estimate the width of the book in centimeters.

_____ cm

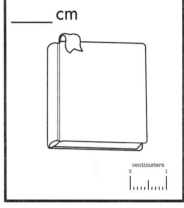

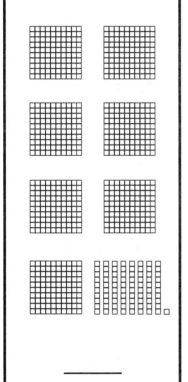

_____

Label the shapes that you see in the drawing.

___ : ___

13 + 7 =

5 quarters and 3 dimes.

$ _____

Write **<**, **>**, or **=** to compare.

292 ◯ 392        880 ◯ 880

890 ◯ 819        992 ◯ 929

551 ◯ 155        365 ◯ 536

Divide the rectangle into 10 equal parts.

Use addition to fill in the pyramid. Each number is the sum of the two numbers below it.

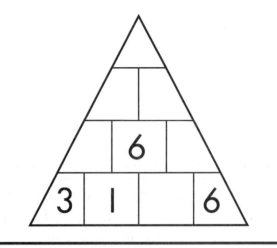

Jack put 24 chocolate chips in cookies and 32 chocolate chips in brownies. If he has 25 chocolate chips left, how many did he start with?

Write **<**, **>**, or **=** to compare.

**880** ◯ **808**

**278** ◯ **278**

**221** ◯ **212**

**365** ◯ **653**

$$\begin{array}{r} 772 \\ -\ 389 \\ \hline \end{array}$$

$$\begin{array}{r} 65 \\ 33 \\ +\ 45 \\ \hline \end{array}$$

Write the missing numbers.

|     | 55  |     |
| --- | --- | --- |
| 64  |     |     |
| 74  |     |     |

| Favorite Exercise | |
| --- | --- |
| Playing ball | 🏃🏃🏃🏃🏃🏃🏃 |
| Dancing | 🏃🏃🏃🏃🏃 |
| Running | 🏃🏃🏃 |
| Jumping | 🏃🏃🏃🏃 |

🏃 = 1 person

How many people liked jumping or dancing? _____

How many more people were playing ball than running? _____

What was the least popular exercise?

_____

**235 + 100 = ____**

**19 − 9 + 10 − 7 =**

**3 + 8 − 5 + 13 =**

Measure the bee to the nearest inch and centimeter.

____ in.

____ cm

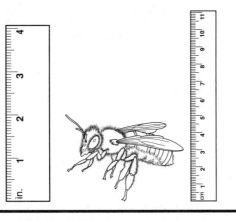

Jasmine had 92¢ in her piggy bank. Then she went for a walk and found a penny and two nickels. How much money does she have now?

Wesley's class shared their favorite breakfast foods. Three like to eat toast. Five like to eat cereal. Two like to eat eggs and bacon best, and two like to eat pancakes. Draw a bar graph to show this.

$$8 + 8 - 5 - 3 =$$

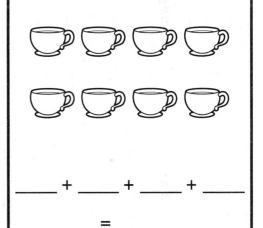

____ + ____ + ____ + ____

= ____

$$
\begin{array}{r}
8\,\square \\
-\ 5\ 2 \\
\hline
3\ 6
\end{array}
$$

Color the shape that has the least number of faces.

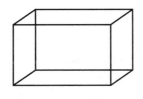

| 335 | | |
|---|---|---|
| Hundreds | Tens | Ones |
| | | |

$$5 + 12 =$$

$$18 - 4 =$$

**889**   **277**   **399**
**− 432**  **− 219**  **+ 176**

Elizabeth had 24 olives. She ate some of them. Now she has 12 olives. How many olives did she eat?

321, _____, _____, 315,

_____, _____

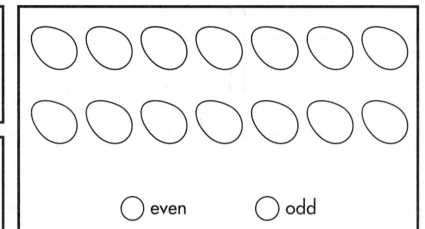

Cross out base ten blocks to subtract.

**672 − 311 = ____**

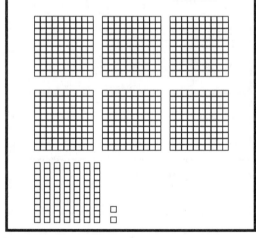

○ even    ○ odd

**15 − 13 =**

Write the number.

eight hundred
fifty-nine

How much longer is one pen than the other?

____ in.

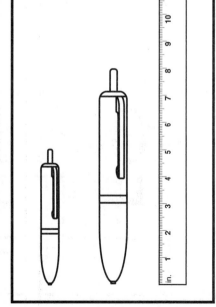

Complete the doubles fact.

____ + ____ = 18

Write the numbers in expanded form.

**355 = _____**

**533 = _____**

| | | | |
|---|---|---|---|
| 10<br>+10 | 20<br>+10 | 30<br>+10 | 40<br>+10 |
| 50<br>+10 | 60<br>+10 | 70<br>+10 | 80<br>+10 |
| 90<br>+10 | 100<br>+10 | 100<br>+20 | 100<br>+30 |
| 100<br>+40 | 100<br>+50 | 100<br>+60 | 100<br>+70 |

| 50 | 40 | 30 | 20 |
|----|----|----|----|
| 90 | 80 | 70 | 60 |
| 130 | 120 | 110 | 100 |
| 170 | 160 | 150 | 140 |

| | | | |
|---|---|---|---|
| 10<br>−10 | 20<br>−10 | 30<br>−10 | 40<br>−10 |
| 50<br>−10 | 60<br>−10 | 70<br>−10 | 80<br>−10 |
| 90<br>−10 | 100<br>−10 | 100<br>−20 | 100<br>−30 |
| 100<br>−40 | 100<br>−50 | 100<br>−75 | 100<br>−100 |

| 30 | 20 | 10 | 0 |
|----|----|----|----|
| 70 | 60 | 50 | 40 |
| 70 | 80 | 90 | 80 |
| 0 | 25 | 50 | 60 |

# Answer Key

**Day 1**

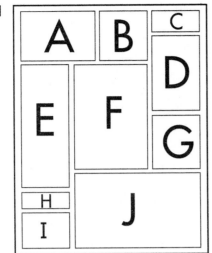

**Day 2**

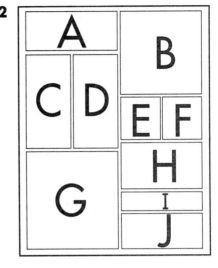

**Day 3**

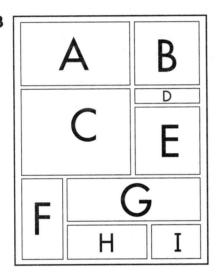

**Day 4**

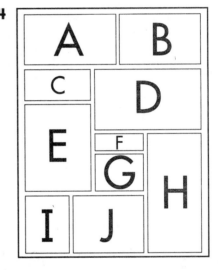

## Week 1, Day 1 (page 17)

A. $3 + 5 + 7 = 15$; B. Check students' work.
C. 16; D. even; E. 2 hundreds, 0 tens, 0 ones;
F. Check students' work. G. Check students' work.
H. 43; I. 8¢; J. 45 < 54, 76 < 77, 52 > 51,
98 < 99, 41 > 31, 87 < 88

## Week 1, Day 2 (page 18)

A. 100; B. $1 + 1 + 1 + 1 = 4$; C. 62 crayons;
D. $5 + 7 = \mathbf{12}$, $\mathbf{7} + 5 = 12$, $12 - \mathbf{5} = 7$,
$\mathbf{12} - 7 = 5$; E. 24; F. 16; G. 5, 3, 16;
H. one hundred forty-three; I. 788;
J. $3 + 2 = 4 + 1$

## Week 1, Day 3 (page 19)

A. 5; B. Check students' work. C. Add, then
subtract. D. 20, 25, 30; E. cube; F. ruler; G. 43¢;
H. 11:45; I. 42

## Week 1, Day 4 (page 20)

A. 93, 79, 59; B. 52 people; C. 8; D. 35; E. 113,
Check students' work. F. 60; G. Check students'
work. H. 3; I. $6 + 6 = 12$; J. $800 + 50 + 3$,
$800 + 50$

## Week 2, Day 1 (page 21)

A. 32; B. one half; C. 343; D. Check students'
work. E. + 11, –15, + 28; F. 4, 7; G. 5 hundreds,
1 ten, 1 one; H. 11; I. ten o'clock; J. Check
students' work.

## Week 2, Day 2 (page 22)

A. four-fourths; B. clockwise from top: 3, 10, 7,
12, 6, 4; C. $3 + 3 + 3 + 3 + 3 = 15$ OR
$5 + 5 + 5 = 15$; D. 45 < 54, 145 > 144,
540 = 540, 450 > 440; E. 500; F. 87; G. 3 in.,
8 cm; H. Students should color the middle box.
I. 303, 313, 323; J. 73

# Answer Key

**Week 2, Day 3 (page 23)**
A. 7 + 3 = 6 + 4, 9 − 5 = 7 − 3, 5 + 2 = 9 − 2,
6 − 1 = 2 + 3; B. 54 − 26; C. 4, 8, 5; D. 13;
E. Check students' work. F. 170; G. Check
students' work. H. 5 hundreds, 0 tens, 9 ones;
I. 600

**Week 2, Day 4 (page 24)**
A. 32, 29, 65; B. four tens; C. 600 + 60 + 3;
D. Marie, Ted, 16; E. Check students' work.
F. 889; G. 732; H. 33; I. 1 inch; J. 45

**Week 3, Day 1 (page 25)**
A. 52; B. 84; C. 8; D. Check students' work.
E. Check students' work. F. Check students' work.
G. Check students' work. H. 30; I. 43¢; J. 11

**Week 3, Day 2 (page 26)**
A. 4; B. 5 + 5 + 5 = 15; C. 90 blocks; D. **5 + 6 =
11, 6 + 5 = 11**, 11 − **6** = 5, **11 − 5 = 6**; E. 42;
F. 40, 100, 80; G. 7, 5, 16; H. fifty-six; I. 499,
500, 501; J. 11, 11

**Week 3, Day 3 (page 27)**
A. 5; B. Check students' work. C. Subtract. Then,
subtract again. D. 20; E. Check students' work.
F. estimates will vary but should be between 1
and 5; G. Check students' work. H. 39 marbles;
I. 764 > 674

**Week 3, Day 4 (page 28)**
A. 44 + **31** = 75, 256 + 242 = 498, 123 + **236**
= 359; B. 65 songs; C. cone; D. 16 animals;
E. 341, Check students' work. F. 10; G. 789; H.
7 cm; I. 4 + 4 = 8; J. 60 + 7,
600 + 70

**Week 4, Day 1 (page 29)**
A. 61 items sold; B. Check students' work.
C. 9; D. odd; E. 13 − 7 = 6, **15 − 9 = 6**, **15 −
8 = 7**, 17 − **8** = **9**, **14** − 5 = **9**, **14** − 6 = 8; F.
Dan, Josie, Harvey and Melissa; G. 9 hundreds,
0 tens, 2 ones; H. 16; I. 5:15; J. 25 < 225, 54 >
45, 137 > 136, 403 > 303, 275 < 285, 800 >
80

**Week 4, Day 2 (page 30)**
A. Check students' work. B. From top to bottom:
20, 11, 9, 5, 3, 2; C. Check students' work.
D. 9 − 5 = 4; E. 302; F. 120; G. 4; H. From top
to bottom: 43, 53, 54, 62, 64; I. 400, 399, 398;
J. 25 feet

**Week 4, Day 3 (page 31)**
A. height of a person = feet, length of a pencil
= inches, length of a field = yards; B. 38 + 51;
C. 3, 5, 11; D. 7 tens, 0 ones; E. sphere; F. 197
− **54** = 143; G. 68¢; H. noon; I. 532, 542, 552

**Week 4, Day 4 (page 32)**
A. 223, 213, 265; B. 364 = 4, 450 = 400, 145
= 40, 904 = 4; C. 501 < 510; D. Ms. Ellis, 4;
E. From top to bottom: 16, 17, 8; F. 4; G. 115;
H. 30 sheets; I. dollar; J. 132

**Week 5, Day 1 (page 33)**
A. 24; B. Check students' work. C. 14; D. ruler;
E. Check students' work. F. circles, rectangles,
square; G. 4:05; H. 701; I. 58¢; J. 8 cm

**Week 5, Day 2 (page 34)**
A. cylinder; B. clockwise from top: 4, 7, 2, 5, 3,
6; C. 77¢; D. 651 > 650, 345 > 245,
301 < 311, 989 > 889; E. 114; F. 36; G. 16, 4,
3; H. Check students' work. I. 750, 748, 747;
J. 4 + 1 = 5

**Week 5, Day 3 (page 35)**
A. 3 cm; B. Check students' work. C. 12 times,
summer; D. 9 tens + 9 ones; E. Check students'
work. F. 80; G. 3; H. 60 stamps; I. 80

**Week 5, Day 4 (page 36)**
A. 9, explanations will vary; B. 90 sit-ups;
C. eight hundred nine; D. Check students' work.
E. From top to bottom: 11, 9, 7, 13, 20; F. 16;
G. Check students' work. H. 17 blueberries;
I. 3 + 3 = 6; J. 300 + 90 + 9, 200 + 30 + 4

**Week 6, Day 1 (page 37)**
A. 93 feet; B. 53; C. 6; D. meters; E. 90, 80, 70,
60, 50; F. tomato, 15, 1; G. 428; H. 17; I. 4:30;
J. check student's work

**Week 6, Day 2 (page 38)**
A. 8 edges, 5 faces, 5 vertices; B. clockwise from
top: 15, 12, 11, 16, 14, 9; C. Check students'
work. D. 34 > 24, 78 < 87, 56 < 57, 46 = 46;
E. 810; F. 20; G. 3 in., 7 cm; H. From top to
bottom: 123, 124, 132, 134, 142; I. 240;
J. 32 roses

**Week 6, Day 3 (page 39)**
A. triangle = 3 sides, 3 angles, quadrilateral = 4
sides, 4 angles, circle = no sides, no angles;
B. 6 − 3 = 3; C. add once, subtract once; D. 15;
E. 2 + 2 + 2 = 6 OR 3 + 3 = 6; F. 7 in.; G. 20,
50, 80; H. 4 hundreds, 7 tens, 6 ones; I. 78 > 67

# Answer Key

## Week 6, Day 4 (page 40)
A. 37 + 5**2** = 89, 41 + **3**8 = 79, 25 + **7**1 = 96;
B. 90; C. 100 + 20; D. Even numbers colored
will reveal a smiley face. E. 111, Check students'
work. F. 90; G. 990; H. 8 cm; I. yard; J. 33

## Week 7, Day 1 (page 41)
A. 13 paint brushes; B. Check students' work.
C. 17; D. even; E. 4 + 5 = **9**, 2 + **7** = **9**,
4 + **7** = **11**, 5 + 6 = **11**, 5 + **3** = 8, 9 + **3** = 12;
F. Check students' work. G. 3:55; H. 14; I. 44¢;
J. 2 hundreds, 1 ten, 4 ones, 200 + 10 + 4,
2 hundreds blocks, 1 tens rod, 4 ones blocks

## Week 7, Day 2 (page 42)
A. Check students' work. B. From top to bottom:
22, 11, 11, 6, 3, 2; C. 18 samosas; D. 3 + 4 =
7, 4 + 3 = 7, 7 – 3 = 4, 7 – 4 = 3; E. 151;
F. 162; G. 3, 3, 4; H. Students should color the
first box. I. 400; J. 8

## Week 7, Day 3 (page 43)
A. 6 cm; B. 54 strawberries; C. 4, baseball
and volleyball, 18; D. 6 tens, 1 one; E. Check
students' work. F. 191 – **7**1 = 120; G. Check
students' work. H. 27 trees; I. 14 – 7 = 7,
7 + 8 = 15

## Week 7, Day 4 (page 44)
A. 27; B. 425 = 20, 203 = 200, 632 = 2,
812 = 2; C. 6; D. 24; E. From top to bottom: 16,
11, 18; F. 100; G. eighteen; H. 66 students; I. 1;
J. 542, 97, 180

## Week 8, Day 1 (page 45)
A. 13; B. 30 ones; C. 19;
D. Check students' work. E. Check students' work.
F. 13, 5, 40; G. 593; H. 60; I. 6:30; J. Check
student's work.

## Week 8, Day 2 (page 46)
A. Check students' work. B. clockwise from top:
6, 10, 8, 12, 9, 13; C. 32 DVDs; D. 811 > 801,
456 > 455, 200 > 190, 730 < 740; E. 897;
F. 5 tens, 4 ones; G. 7 cm; H. seven hundred
thirty-eight; I. 251, 250, 248; J. 7 = 3 + 4

## Week 8, Day 3 (page 47)
A. 455 = four hundred fifty-five, four hundred
sixty-five = 400 + 60 + 5, 500 + 40 + 6 = 546;
B. Check students' work. C. Add. Then, subtract.
D. 12; E. 5 + 5 + 5 + 5 + 5 = 25; F. 1 foot;
G. 17 – 8; H. seven twenty; I. 400

## Week 8, Day 4 (page 48)
A. 81, 38, 87; B. 39 songs; C. 600 + 80; D. 14,
6 more sparrows; E. From top to bottom: 10, 2,
15, 7, 8; F. 9; G. Check students' work. H. 12
cm; I. Check students' work. J. 22

## Week 9, Day 1 (page 49)
A. 28 cookies; B. Check students' work. C. 4;
D. Students should color the middle box. E. + 23,
+ 41, – 54; F. 3, 3, 12; G. Check students' work.
H. 69; I. 22¢; J. 567 > 566; 802 > 702,
311 = 311, 231 > 221, 607 < 617, 488 > 480

## Week 9, Day 2 (page 50)
A. 2 faces; B. 5 + 5 + 5 + 5 = 20; C. 62 peas; D.
8 + 9 = 17, 9 + 8 = 17, 17 – 8 = 9, 17 – 9
= 8; E. 102; F. 75; G. Morgan, Jared and
Britney, Vincent; H. From top to bottom: 348,
349, 357, 359, 367, 368; I. 699, 599, 499;
J. 34 feet

## Week 9, Day 3 (page 51)
A. 5 in., 12 cm; B. triangle; C. Hilary, Jose,
6 scoops; D. 8 tens, 9 ones; E. Check students'
work. F. 117; G. 84¢; H. 3 hundreds, 0 tens,
1 one; I. 25 < 35

## Week 9, Day 4 (page 52)
A. 728, 154, 655; B. 426 = 6, 162 = 60,
640 = 600, 706 = 6; C. five hundred eighty;
D. 4 + 2 = 6; E. 24, Check students' work.
F. 402; G. twenty-seven; H. 74 items;
I. 4 + 4 = 8; J. 460, 406, 416

## Week 10, Day 1 (page 53)
A. 37 chips; B. 109; C. 18; D. meters; E. 9 + 7
= **16**, 8 + 8 = **16**, 8 + 3 = **11**, **2** + 9 = **11**,
**2** + **10** = 12, 10 + **10** = 20; F. Check students'
work. G. 1; H. 7; I. 11:05; J. 3 cm

## Week 10, Day 2 (page 54)
A. Check students' work. B. From top to bottom:
20, 11, 9, 5, 4, 1; C. 59; D. 750 > 550; 321 >
320, 873 > 863, 428 > 389; E. 634; F. 123;
G. 6 cm; H. three hundred fifty-three; I. 483;
J. 20

## Week 10, Day 3 (page 55)
A. cube, square, cone; B. 13;
C. Add. Then subtract. D. 19; E. Check students'
work. F. 193; G. 70, Check students' work.
H. two fifteen OR quarter past two; I. 340 < 420

# Answer Key

## Week 10, Day 4 (page 56)
A. 384, 641, 778; B. 190 = 90, 532 = 2, 426 = 20, 377 = 300; C. 850, 840, 830; D. 1; E. From top to bottom: 11, 7, 5; F. 9; G. Check students' work. H. 2 cm; I. 1 cm; J. 300 + 60, 400 + 30 + 3

## Week 11, Day 1 (page 57)
A. 84 tires; B. Check students' work. C. 17; D. odd; E. 424; F. monkeys, elephants, 8; G. 11:25; H. 633; I. 80¢; J. three hundred eight, 3 hundreds, 0 tens, 8 ones, 3 hundreds blocks and 8 ones blocks

## Week 11, Day 2 (page 58)
A. 6 faces, 12 edges, 8 vertices; B. clockwise from top: 14, 16, 11, 13, 15, 12; C. Check students' work. D. 3 + 6 = 9, 6 + 3 = 9, 9 – 3 = 6, 9 – 6 = 3; E. 93; F. 4 hundreds, 4 tens, 1 one; G. 5 cm, 1 cm, 0 caterpillars; H. Students should color the middle box. I. 685, 690, 695; J. 23

## Week 11, Day 3 (page 59)
A. 2 in., 6 cm; B. 88 – 34; C. 1 more, water and juice, 15; D. 5; E. Check students' work. F. 77 – 53 = 24; G. 36¢; H. 7 hundreds, 2 tens, 7 ones; I. 350 > 340

## Week 11, Day 4 (page 60)
A. 33 blocks; B. 324 = 300, 535 = 30, 370 = 300, 893 = 3; C. four hundred forty; D. 12 – 4 = 8; E. From top to bottom: 11, 7, 9, 9, 18; F. 312; G. sixty hundred twenty-two; H. 46 T-shirts; I. Check students' work. J. 91, 24

## Week 12, Day 1 (page 61)
A. 15 seeds; B. 109; C. 4; D. 1 inch; E. 230, 235, 240, 245, 250; F. 1 circle, 1 rectangle, 2 triangles, and 1 trapezoid; G. 6 hundreds, 6 tens, 4 ones; H. 20; I. 9:35; J. 6 in., 16 cm

## Week 12, Day 2 (page 62)
A. pyramid; B. clockwise from top: 9, 5, 12, 4, 10, 7; C. 3 + 3 + 3 + 3 + 3 = 15 OR 5 + 5 + 5 = 15; D. 555 > 554, 242 < 252, 304 > 294, 112 = 112; E. 36; F. 143; G. 2 cm; H. seven hundred seventy-seven; I. 118, 117, 116; J. 15 in.

## Week 12, Day 3 (page 63)
A. cube = 6, pyramid = 5, cylinder = 1, cone = 1; B. 30¢; C. penguins, 3, 5; D. 12; E. trapezoid; F. 140; G. Check students' work. H. six fifteen OR quarter past six; I. 20, 1

## Week 12, Day 4 (page 64)
A. 18, 27, 32; B. 13 in.; C. 500 + 90; D. 6 + 4 = 10; E. From top to bottom: 4, 11, 6; F. 4; G. 329; H. 11 cm; I. 4 in.; J. 398, 563, 422

## Week 13, Day 1 (page 65)
A. 11 cupcakes; B. three-fourths; C. 210; D. even; E. + 37, – 43, + 32; F. 4, 6, 24 cookies; G. 8:25; H. 367; I. 76¢; J. 354 < 454, 276 > 267, 511 > 510, 499 < 509, 899 < 901, 933 < 934

## Week 13, Day 2 (page 66)
A. 205; B. 4 + 4 + 4 = 12; C. 43 items; D. 2 + 7 = 9, 7 + 2 = 9, 9 – 7 = 2, 9 – 2 = 7; E. 331; F. 132; G. 3 in.; H. From top to bottom: 154, 156, 164, 165, 175, 176; I. 875, 873, 872; J. 4 – 3 = 1

## Week 13, Day 3 (page 67)
A. 5 in.; B. Check students' work. C. Subtract. Then, subtract again. D. 13; E. Check students' work. F. 176 – 46 = 130; G. 25; H. 59 insects; I. 359 > 329

## Week 13, Day 4 (page 68)
A. 36 vegetables; B. 32 parking spaces; C. 5; D. 11 ducks; E. 131, Check students' work. F. 452; G. 201; H. 7 in.; I. 5 + 5 = 10; J. 263, 478

## Week 14, Day 1 (page 69)
A. 12 in.; B. 120; C. 3; D. 3 cm; E. 20 – 10 = 10, 15 – 5 = 10, 13 – 5 = 8, 17 – 9 = 8, 16 – 9 = 7, 16 – 8 = 8; F. 2, Wednesday, 2 squirrels; G. Check students' work. H. 650; I. 35¢; J. one hundred thirty-three, 1 hundred, 3 tens, 3 ones, 100 + 30 + 3

## Week 14, Day 2 (page 70)
A. Check students' work. B. From top to bottom: 26, 13, 13, 7, 6, 3; C. 56 pepperoni; D. 340 < 360, 278 < 280, 542 = 542, 364 < 370; E. 843; F. 135; G. 2, 3, 10; H. Students should color the middle box. I. 788; J. 9

## Week 14, Day 3 (page 71)
A. 3 in., 7 cm; B. three thirds; C. Manuel, Diana, 15; D. 8; E. Check students' work. F. 186; G. Check students' work. H. 7 hundreds, 1 ten, 4 ones; I. 300

# Answer Key

**Week 14, Day 4 (page 72)**
A. 234, 889, 81; B. 40 in.; C. 400 + 30 + 9;
D. 5 + 3 = 8; E. From top to bottom: 7, 3, 8, 4,
4; F. 898; G. 651; H. 22 balls; I. 2 cm; J. 200
+ 20 + 2, 900 + 30 + 9

**Week 15, Day 1 (page 73)**
A. 29 umbrellas; B. 111; C. 10; D. odd;
E. 2 hundreds blocks, 6 tens rods, 1 ones block;
F. 4, 3; G. 12:35; H. 17; I. 95¢; J. 4 in.

**Week 15, Day 2 (page 74)**
A. Check students' work. B. Clockwise from top:
10, 8, 7, 12, 9, 11, 13, 6; C. $22;
D. 356 < 456, 299 > 280, 545 < 550, 713
> 703; E. 46; F. 162; G. mint, 3, 2; H. Check
students' work. I. 62, 72, 82; J. 6 + 9 = 15

**Week 15, Day 3 (page 75)**
A. Check students' matches. B. Check students'
work. C. addition and subtraction; D. 3; E. 3 + 3
= 6 OR 2 + 2 + 2 = 6; F. 182; G. Check students'
work. H. 4 hundreds, 3 tens, 3 ones; I. 5, 15

**Week 15, Day 4 (page 76)**
A. 22, 24, 29; B. 431 = 400, 89 = 80,
532 = 30, 381 = 1; C. Check students' work.
D. 31, Explanations will vary. E. From top to
bottom: 14, 9, 7; F. 18; G. 745; H. 9 in.;
I. Check students' work. J. 129, 372, 484

**Week 16, Day 1 (page 77)**
A. 84 items; B. Check students' work. C. 17; D.
11 cm; E. 250, 350, 450, 550, 650; F. Check
students' work. G. 6 hundreds, 0 tens, 7 ones; H.
322; I. 12:40; J. Check student's work.

**Week 16, Day 2 (page 78)**
A. cube; B. 5 + 5 + 5 + 5 = 20; C. 25¢;
D. 11 – 4 = 4; E. 809; F. 185; G. 12, sailboats
and fishing boats, 3; H. From top to bottom: 55,
57, 66; I. 334; J. 38 berries

**Week 16, Day 3 (page 79)**
A. Estimates should be between 3 and 5 inches.
B. 61 + 34; C. Steven, 3; D. 9; E. Check students'
work. F. 87 – 46 = 41; G. $9; H. two twenty-
five; I. 571 > 561

**Week 16, Day 4 (page 80)**
A. 25 + 64 = 89, 42 + 34 = 76, 19 + 60 = 79;
B. 40; C. 7; D. 14 – 5 = 9; E. Check students'
work. F. 9; G. pentagon; H. 14 cm; I. 6, Check
students' work. J. 798, 554

**Week 17, Day 1 (page 81)**
A. 75 bottles of water; B. 103; C. 3; D. Check
students' work. E. – 21, + 62, – 55; F. 4, 2, 1;
G. 4 hundreds, 4 tens, 9 ones; H. 20; I. 3:35.
J. 2 hundreds, 4 tens, 2 ones, 200 + 40 + 2, 2
hundreds blocks, 4 tens rods, 2 ones blocks.

**Week 17, Day 2 (page 82)**
A. 6; B. From top to bottom: 20, 12, 8, 4, 6, 2;
C. 12 feet; D. 377 < 380, 212 < 221,
414 < 440, 870 < 910; E. 99; F. 82; G. 3, 2,
13; H. one hundred twenty-nine; I. 455; J. 13

**Week 17, Day 3 (page 83)**
A. Check students' matches. B. 94¢; C. 15, 3, 26;
D. 705; E. Check students' work. F. 157;
G. 15 + 30; H. eight twenty; I. 530 > 529

**Week 17, Day 4 (page 84)**
A. 94, 88, 81; B. 84¢; C. 800 + 20 + 5;
D. Students should color the first tree. E. From top
to bottom: 17, 3, 10, 10, 20; F. 772; G. 313;
H. 15; I. 7 + 7 = 14; J. 25

**Week 18, Day 1 (page 85)**
A. 26 sides; B. 18; C. 2; D. 2 in.; E. 11 – 2
= **9**, 5 + 4 = **9**, 5 – 3 = 2, 8 + **3** = 11,
15 – **4** = **11**, 8 + 4 = 12; F. cones and cylinders;
G. 6:55; H. 20; I. 55¢; J. 355 < 360,
890 > 880, 546 < 456, 244 > 243, 555 < 556,
342 < 442

**Week 18, Day 2 (page 86)**
A. Check students' work. B. Clockwise from top:
9, 13, 10, 11, 7, 8, 12, 6; C. Check students'
work. D. 8 + 9 = 17, 9 + 8 = 17, 17 – 8 = 9, 17
– 9 = 8; E. 810; F. 105; G. 16, 8, 48; H. four
hundred fifty; I. 430, 420, 410; J. 57 insects

**Week 18, Day 3 (page 87)**
A. 5 in., 12 cm; B. 56¢; C. 3, 5, 2; D. 15;
E. 1 + 1 + 1 + 1 = 4; F. **8**9 – 53 = 36; G. Check
students' work. H. 8 hundreds, 9 tens, 9 ones;
I. 10, 12

**Week 18, Day 4 (page 88)**
A. 212, 496, 223; B. 13 mints; C. 600, 602,
603; D. even; E. 121, Check students' work. F. 6;
G. 970; H. 2 in.; I. 8 + 8 = 16; J. 400 + 60,
300 + 90 + 9

# Answer Key

**Week 19, Day 1 (page 89)**
A. 13 people; B. two-fourths; C. 513;
D. Estimates should be between 1 and 3 cm.
E. 605, 610, 615, 620; F. 6, 5, 3; G. Check
students' work. H. 600; I. 96¢; J. 5 in., 13 cm

**Week 19, Day 2 (page 90)**
A. 300; B. Check students' work. C. 47 in.;
D. 455 < 555, 323 = 323, 247 > 237, 110 =
110; E. 825; F. 149; G. Ursula, Marty and Elena,
11; H. From top to bottom: 278, 279, 286, 287;
I. 496, 396, 296; J. 19

**Week 19, Day 3 (page 91)**
A. 12 cm; B. 33 in.; C. addition and subtraction;
D. 15; E. prism; F. 198; G. Check students' work.
H. eight twenty-five; I. 2, 18

**Week 19, Day 4 (page 92)**
A. 46 + 43 = 89, 28 + 71 = 99, 52 + 38 = 90;
B. 508 = 8, 877 = 800, 283 = 80, 980 = 80;
C. 340 > 339; D. 11 – 3 = 8; E. From top to
bottom: 18, 14, 5; F. 820; G. 202; H. $12;
I. 1 yard; J. 19, 21

**Week 20, Day 1 (page 93)**
A. 8 glasses; B. 88; C. 1; D. Check students'
work. E. – 24, – 31, + 48; F. 6 in., 7 in., 16;
G. Check students' work. H. 344; I. 36¢; J. one
hundred eighty-five, 1 hundred, 8 tens, 5 ones, 1
hundreds block, 8 tens rods, 5 ones blocks

**Week 20, Day 2 (page 94)**
A. Check students' work. B. Check students' work.
C. 43¢; D. 8 – 11 = 3; E. 34; F. 116; G. 3 in.;
H. five hundred sixty-five; I. 780, 779, 778; J. 6

**Week 20, Day 3 (page 95)**
A. Check students' matches. B. 77 coloring tools;
C. 7, 3; D. 12; E. Check students' work. F. 254;
G. 50; H. 3 hundreds, 8 tens, 3 ones;
I. 609 < 709

**Week 20, Day 4 (page 96)**
A. 23 pieces; B. 555 = 50, 820 = 0, 330 = 300,
209 = 200; C. 700 + 90; D. even; E. 102, Check
students' work. F. 973; G. 0 faces; H. 83¢;
I. 3 + 3 = 6; J. 676, 734

**Week 21, Day 1 (page 97)**
A. 35 gallons; B. 1 hundred, 1 ten; C. 20;
D. Check students' work. E. 18 – 9 = 9,
17 – 8 = 9, 12 – 8 = 4, 11 – 7 = 4,
15 – 7 = 8, 16 – 8 = 8; F. 10, 10, 30; G. 6:35;
H. 76; I. 75¢; J. 16 cm, 6 in.

**Week 21, Day 2 (page 98)**
A. thirds; B. Clockwise from top: 17, 13, 16, 18,
11, 15, 12, 14; C. 38¢; D. 797 > 790,
380 > 370, 422 < 522, 337 < 338; E. 22;
F. 102; G. Maria, 14, Eli and Rosa; H. three
hundred sixty; I. 698, 688, 678; J. 14

**Week 21, Day 3 (page 99)**
A. Check students' matches. B. 73 – 45; C. Check
students' work. D. 390; E. pyramid; F. 154;
G. 75¢; H. 7 hundreds, 0 tens, 1 one; I. 20, 1

**Week 21, Day 4 (page 100)**
A. 92, 75, 85; B. 90; C. seven hundred seventy;
D. 5, Explanations will vary. E. Check students'
work. F. 443; G. 555; H. 61 drink choices; I. 3
cm; J. 43, 18

**Week 22, Day 1 (page 101)**
A. 22 T-shirts; B. 32; C. 236; D. 1 meter; E. 538;
F. trapezoid, hexagon, pentagon, square; G. 6
hundreds, 6 tens, 8 ones; H. 8; I. 3:20; J. Check
student's work.

**Week 22, Day 2 (page 102)**
A. Check students' work. B. From top to bottom:
20, 11, 9, 6, 4, 1; C. 5 + 5 = 10 OR 2 + 2 + 2
+ 2 + 2 = 10; D. 6 + 1 = 7, 1 + 6 = 7, 7 – 1 = 6,
7 – 6 = 1; E. 635; F. 254; G. 6 cm; H. From top
to bottom: 445, 454, 456, 465; I. 678;
J. 5 – 1 = 4

**Week 22, Day 3 (page 103)**
A. 5 in.; B. 53¢; C. 90 – 69 – 12; D. 9; E. Check
students' work. F. 489 – 156 = 333; G. Check
students' work. H. eight fifty; I. 888 < 988

**Week 22, Day 4 (page 104)**
A. 46 – 31 = 15, 58 – 17 = 41, 73 – 42 = 31;
B. 88 marbles; C. trapezoid; D. 5 – 2 = 3;
E. From top to bottom: 7, 3, 8; F. 681; G. 799;
H. 18 shoes; I. 10 + 10 = 20; J. 300 + 6,
200 + 20 + 8

**Week 23, Day 1 (page 105)**
A. 42 toys; B. Check students' work. C. 4;
D. odd; E. 735, 745, 755, 765, 775; F. olives,
3, 5; G. Check students' work. H. 242; I. 85¢;
J. one hundred sixty-three, 1 hundred, 6 tens, 3
ones, 100 + 60 + 3

# Answer Key

**Week 23, Day 2 (page 106)**
A. 5 sides, 5 angles; B. Clockwise from top: 7, 15, 8, 6, 11, 13, 9, 12; C. 7 feet; D. 644 > 633, 272 > 270, 399 < 599, 405 < 415; E. 52; F. 108; G. 4 in., 10 cm; H. five hundred five; I. 649, 648, 647; J. 44

**Week 23, Day 3 (page 107)**
A. Check students' matches. B. $35; C. 3, Cameron, 25; D. 12; E. 4 + 4 + 4 = 12 OR 3 + 3 + 3 + 3 = 12; F. 164; G. 57¢; H. 6 hundreds, 6 tens, 4 ones; I. 20, 13

**Week 23, Day 4 (page 108)**
A. 91, 18, 23; B. 37 scarves; C. 522 > 512; D. 12, 5, 37; E. From top to bottom: 12, 2, 13, 3, 10; F. 690; G. 553; H. 16 cm; I. 1 + 1 = 2; J. 24

**Week 24, Day 1 (page 109)**
A. 53 crayons; B. 70; C. 420; D. 5 cm; E. + 14, – 26, + 31; F. 6, 1, 23; G. 3 hundreds, 4 tens, 4 ones; H. 682; I. 6:45; J. 256 < 266, 387 < 487, 499 = 499, 301 < 305, 644 > 634, 708 < 808

**Week 24, Day 2 (page 110)**
A. 154; B. Clockwise from top: 19, 10, 16, 14, 17, 13, 15, 12; C. 38¢; D. 2 – 6 = 4; E. 353; F. 136; G. 1 inch; H. Students should color the middle ice cream cone. I. 201, 200, 199; J. 17.

**Week 24, Day 3 (page 111)**
A. 3 cm; B. 21; C. 8, 2, building blocks; D. 360; E. 8 pieces; F. 197; H. 57; I. 95 animals; J. 2, 14

**Week 24, Day 4 (page 112)**
A. 38 pies; B. 771 = 700, 770 = 70, 669 = 9, 668 = 600; C. 300 + 9; D. 42, Explanations will vary. E. 122, Check students' work. F. 667; G. 901; H. 47 shells; I. 2 + 2 = 4; J. 132, 878

**Week 25, Day 1 (page 113)**
A. 54; B. Check students' work. C. 356; D. Check students' work. E. 7 + 3 = **10**, **6** + 4 = **10**, **6** + 2 = 8, 9 + **2** = **11**, 8 + 3 = **11**, 8 + 7 = 15; F. 2, 6, 4; G. Check students' work. H. 496; I. 81¢; J. 5 in.

**Week 25, Day 2 (page 114)**
A. 5 faces, 9 edges, 6 vertices; B. From top to bottom: 20, 13, 7, 3, 8, 1; C. 8 feet; D. 2 + 8 = 10, 8 + 2 = 10, 10 – 8 = 2, 10 – 2 = 8; E. 729; F. 338; G. 9 cm; H. From top to bottom: 878, 888, 889; I. 899; J. 4

**Week 25, Day 3 (page 115)**
A. 3 in., 8 cm; B. 45¢; C. Check students' work. D. 903; E. 6; F. **78** – **37** = 41; G. 90 – 30; H. twelve fifteen OR quarter past twelve; I. 352

**Week 25, Day 4 (page 116)**
A. 122, 193, 172; B. 27; C. seventy-nine; D. odd; E. From top to bottom: 4, 5, 7; F. 535; G. 814; H. Charlie; I. 3 + 3 = 6; J. 553, 242, 780, 601

**Week 26, Day 1 (page 117)**
A. 27 in. ; B. 15; C. 391; D. 6 cm; E. + 25, – 27, – 20; F. 3, 6, 13; G. 5 hundreds, 0 tens, 0 ones; H. 12; I. 93¢; J. two hundred sixty-two, 200 + 60 + 2, 2 hundreds blocks, 6 tens rods, 2 ones blocks

**Week 26, Day 2 (page 118)**
A. Check students' work. B. Clockwise from top: 2, 3, 7, 5, 9, 4, 6, 11; C. 14 pillows; D. 810 > 808, 435 < 440, 366 > 266, 812 < 813; E. 273; F. 173; G. 2 in., 6 cm; H. six hundred two; I. 713, 703, 693; J. 54

**Week 26, Day 3 (page 119)**
A. Check students' matches. B. 92¢; C. 40 – 20 + 14; D. 11; E. 6 sides, 6 angles; F. 120; G. 56¢; H. eleven ten; I. 12, 9

**Week 26, Day 4 (page 120)**
A. 89 – 3**7** = 52, **67** – 24 = 43, **76** – 23 = 53; B. 30 chairs; C. 900 + 70 + 1; D. 3 + 7 = 10; E. From top to bottom: 20, 5, 12, 13, 25; F. 249; G. 505; H. 14 cm; I. 8 + 8 = 16; J. 601, 757

**Week 27, Day 1 (page 121)**
A. 17 cherries; B. three fourths; C. 886; D. even; E. 585, 575, 565, 555, 545; F. 15, 20; G. 5:55; H. 652; I. 78¢; J. 89 < 809, 314 > 159, 602 > 236, 124 <125, 308 = 308, 535 < 585

**Week 27, Day 2 (page 122)**
A. 9 pieces; B. Clockwise from top: 19, 11, 17, 12, 16, 13, 18, 10; C. 9 melons; D. 8 + 10 = 18; E. 337; F. 111; G. 3, 2; H. From top to bottom: 337, 346, 348, 357; I. 437; J. 13

**Week 27, Day 3 (page 123)**
A. Estimates should be between 4 and 6 inches. B. 46 – 32; C. Check students' work. D. 11; E. Check students' work. F. 145; G. Check students' work. H. 4 hundreds, 6 tens, 0 ones; I. 18, 4

# Answer Key

**Week 27, Day 4 (page 124)**
A. 932, 135, 954; B. 38 pieces; C. 11, 11;
D. building a snowman, 11, 5; E. Check students'
work. F. 310; G. trapezoid; H. $2 and 11¢;
I. odd; J. 87, 9

**Week 28, Day 1 (page 125)**
A. 30 cousins; B. 62; C. 418; D. even; E. 8 + **6**
= 14, 16 − **6** = **10**, 5 + 5 = **10**, 12 − **5** = **7**,
3 + **4** = **7**, 13 − **4** = 9; F. 6, 5, 5; G. Check
students' work. H. 4; I. 34¢; J. 4 in., 9 cm

**Week 28, Day 2 (page 126)**
A. 0 faces, 0 edges, 0 vertices; B. From top to
bottom: 20, 12, 8, 6, 6, 1; C. 63 meters; D. 570
< 670, 344 > 343, 226 > 216, 980 > 975; E.
81; F. 109; G. 9 cm; H. two hundred ninety-four;
I. 80, 70, 60; J. 69

**Week 28, Day 3 (page 127)**
A. 2 cm; B. 43 juice boxes; C. Check students'
work. D. 870; E. 20; F. 128; G. 63¢; H. nine ten;
I. 16, 5

**Week 28, Day 4 (page 128)**
A. 92, 26, 26; B. 1; C. 212 < 312; D. 11 − 4
= 7; E. From top to bottom: 18, 16, 11; F. 18;
G. 290; H. 28 in.; I. 1 cm; J. 382, 574, 199

**Week 29, Day 1 (page 129)**
A. 36 keys; B. Check students' work. C. 444;
D. odd; E. + 24, − 35, + 17; F. Check students'
work. G. 3:20; H. 777; I. 51¢; J. 1 cm

**Week 29, Day 2 (page 130)**
A. 12; B. 18, 13, 11, 12, 14, 16, 10, 15; C. 25
yards; D. 4 + 2 = 6, 2 + 4 = 6, 6 − 4 = 2, 6 − 2
= 4; E. 17; F. 407; G. 5 in., 13 cm; H. From top
to bottom: 202, 211, 212; I. 445, 345, 245;
J. 22

**Week 29, Day 3 (page 131)**
A. Estimates should be between 3 and 5 cm.
B. $2 and 70¢; C. 25 − 14; D. 13; E. Check
students' work. F. 2 cm; G. Check students' work.
H. 3 hundreds, 2 tens, 8 ones; I. 241 < 441

**Week 29, Day 4 (page 132)**
A. **54** − 21 = 33, **64** − 32 = 32, **45** − 34 = 11;
B. 93 miles; C. 600 + 80; D. 8, 8, 2; E. From top
to bottom: 10, 11, 13, 8, 21; F. 415; G. 820;
H. 22 crickets; I. 3 + 3 = 6, 4 + 4 = 8, 5 + 5
= 10; J. 70, 35

**Week 30, Day 1 (page 133)**
A. 25 hairclips; B. Check students' work. C. 102
< 201; D. 4 + 4 + 4 = 12; E. 2 inches; F. Check
students' work. G. 167; H. 18; I. 860; J. Jocelyn

**Week 30, Day 2 (page 134)**
A. 3 feet; B. eraser, 1 in.; C. Check students'
work. D. 3:25; E. 27; F. 353; G. 30; H. 7 in.; I.
667; J. 15 + 2 = 17

**Week 30, Day 3 (page 135)**
Check students' matches. B. Check students' work.
C. Check students' work. D. 40 E. From top to
bottom: 76, 85, 87, 95, 96, 97; F. 162; G. 10;
H. 2 hundreds 0 tens 9 ones; I. 521 > 384

**Week 30, Day 4 (page 136)**
A. 11, 60, 47; B. 63 pages; C. A cube has six
faces. D. Check students' work. E. 330; F. 587;
G. 921; H. Check students' work. I. 8; J. 50 + 3,
300 + 5

**Week 31, Day 1 (page 137)**
A. 220¢; B. Check students' work. C. 35;
D. odd; E. 445, 450, 455, 460, 465; F. 4, 1, 3;
G. Check students' work. H. 24; I. 5 hundreds, 2
tens, 9 ones; J. 298 < 398, 888 > 777,
105 < 501, 920 > 392, 485 < 486, 715 < 751

**Week 31, Day 2 (page 138)**
A. pentagon; B. 352; C. Check students' work.
D. <, >, >, <; E. 506; F. 132; G. Clockwise from
top: 4, 11, 8, 13, 7, 5; H. eight hundred twenty-
one; I. 421; J. 50

**Week 31, Day 3 (page 139)**
A. 3 in.; B. 51 + 24; C. 5, 5, 2; D. 8 hundreds, 7
tens, 6 ones; E. Check students' work. F. 1;
G. 20; H. 80¢; I. >

**Week 31, Day 4 (page 140)**
A. 42 decorations; B. 328 = 20, 152 = 2, 290
= 200, 102 = 2; C. three hundred seventy; D.
Check students' work. E. Check students' work.
F. 143; G. thirty-five; H. 64 items; I. 5 + 3 = 8;
J. 260, 216, 206

**Week 32, Day 1 (page 141)**
A. 14; B. Check students' work. C. <; D. 2 + 2 +
2 = 6; E. 4 cm; F. Check students' work. G. 179;
H. 20; I. 470; J. last week

# Answer Key

**Week 32, Day 2 (page 142)**
A. Check students' work. B. From top to bottom: 93, 46, 47, 23, 23, 24, 11, 12, 11, 13; C. 5 + 5 + 5 + 5 + 5 = 25; D. <, <, <, =; E. 194; F. 2 hundreds, 8 tens, 7 ones; G. 3 in.; H. 11, 16, 15; I. 542; J. 34 animals

**Week 32, Day 3 (page 143)**
A. height of a second grader = feet, length of a banana = inches, height of a building = meters; B. Check students' work. C. Check students' work. D. 50; E. From top to bottom: 23, 25, 34, 35, 43, 44; F. 162; G. 2; H. three fifty-five; I. 198 < 809

**Week 32, Day 4 (page 144)**
A. 623, 431, 926; B. 206 = 6, 445 = 400, 983 = 3, 235 = 30; C. 6; D. odd; E. From top to bottom: 70, 31, 39, 13, 18, 21, 7, 6, 12, 9; F. 8; G. Check students' work. H. 9 ft.; I. 10 feet; J. 200 + 30 + 8, 300 + 1

**Week 33, Day 1 (page 145)**
A. 84 items; B. Check students' work. C. 17; D. 322, 639; E. 190, 290, 390, 490, 590; F. Check students' work. G. 5 hundreds, 3 tens, 2 ones; H. 19; I. Check students' work. J. Check students' work.

**Week 33, Day 2 (page 146)**
A. 27; B. Check students' work. C. Check students' work. D. 11:50; E. 52; F. 181; G. 25; H. 6 in.; I. 185, 180, 175; J. 6 + 12 = 18

**Week 33, Day 3 (page 147)**
A. 4 cm; B. 81 + 19; C. 1, 1, 2; D. 3 tens, 5 ones; E. Check students' work. F. 58 − 33 = 25; G. 60; H. 85¢; I. 533 = 533

**Week 33, Day 4 (page 148)**
A. 113, 136, 101; B. 82 blocks; C. Check students' work. D. triangle = 15, circle = 25; E. Check students' work. F. 143; G. 435; H. 42 baked goods; I. Check students' work. J. 420, 432, 343

**Week 34, Day 1 (page 149)**
A. 18; B. 230; C. 8; D. odd; E. 3 hundreds blocks, 2 tens rods, 2 ones blocks; F. 13, 1; G. 12:05; H. 15; I. 95¢; J. two hundred fifty-one, 2 hundreds, 5 tens, 1 one; 200 + 50 + 1

**Week 34, Day 2 (page 150)**
A. 463; B. 2 + 2 + 2 + 2 + 2 = 10; C. 86; D. 9 + 3 = 12, 3 + 9 = 12, 12 − 9 = 3, 12 − 3 = 9; E. 289; F. 128. G. 30; H. two hundred thirty nine; I. 320, 300, 290; J. 39 sandwiches

**Week 34, Day 3 (page 151)**
Check students' matches. B. Check students' work. C. Check students' work. D. 160; E. 3 + 3 + 3 + 3 + 3 = 15 OR 5 + 5 + 5 = 15; F. 170; G. 5 muffins; H. 4 hundreds 7 tens 3 ones; I. 299 < 901

**Week 34, Day 4 (page 152)**
A. 752, 229, 676; B. 103 = 100, 229 = 20, 821 = 1, 235 = 200; C. 600; D. 5 + 5 = 10, 3 + 3 = 6, 4 + 4 = 8; E. From top to bottom: 68, 35, 33, 17, 18, 15, 9, 8, 10, 5; F. 28; G. Check students' work. H. 24 ft.; I. 4 yards; J. 900 + 10 + 1, 300 + 10 + 3

**Week 35, Day 1 (page 153)**
A. 4; B. three-fourths; C. 180; D. 4 cm; E. 200, 300, 400, 500; F. elm, 1; G. Check students' work. H. 400; I. 210¢; J. 4 in., 10 cm

**Week 35, Day 2 (page 154)**
A. Check students' work. B. Check students' work. C. 77¢; D. 11 − 15 = 4; E. 5; F. 86; G. 3:55; H. eight hundred; I. 775, 770, 765; J. 27, 10

**Week 35, Day 3 (page 155)**
A. 10 cm; B. 84 + 34; C. 4, 3, 2; D. 3; E. Check students' work. F. 83 − 42 = 2; G. $7.25; H. six thirty-five; I. 257 > 256

**Week 35, Day 4 (page 156)**
A. 66 + 23 = 89, 21 + 78 = 99, 59 + 35 + 94; B. 832 = 800, 208 = 8, 118 = 8, 181 = 80; C. <; D. Check students' work. E. Clockwise from top: 9, 11, 6, 9, 7, 10; F. 40; G. 416; H. $4.22; I. 15 inches; J. 35, 4

**Week 36, Day 1 (page 157)**
A. 53; B. 838; C. 4; D. Check students' work. E. − 52, + 11, − 22; F. 3, monkey, monkey; G. Check students' work. H. 359; I. 86¢; J. three hundred twenty-four, 3 hundreds 2 tens 4 ones, 300 + 20 + 4

# Answer Key

**Week 36, Day 2 (page 158)**
A. Check students' work. B. Clockwise from top: 9, 12, 9, 8, 10, 11, 15, 13, 14, 7; C. Check students' work. D. 5 + 6 = 11, 6 + 5 = 11, 11 – 6 = 5, 11 – 5 = 6; E. 358; F. 152; G. 20, 35, breads; H. four hundred fifty; I. 430, 420, 410; J. 56

**Week 36, Day 3 (page 159)**
A. Check students' work. B. 117¢; C. addition and subtraction; D. 3 hundreds, 9 tens, 7 ones; E. Check students' work. F. 100; G. 30 – 10; H. seven twenty; I. 251 > 215

**Week 36, Day 4 (page 160)**
A. 14 blueberries; B. 366 = 336 = 6, 663 = 60, 633 = 30, 300; C. 400 + 80 + 7, D.Check students' work. E. 281; F. 378; G. pentagon; H. $1.51; I. 2 + 2 = 4; J. 566, 899

**Week 37, Day 1 (page 161)**
A. 57; B. Check students' work. C. 17; D. 434; E. 190, 290, 390, 490, 590; F. Check students' work. G. 9 hundreds, 8 tens, 2 ones; H. 19; I. Check students' work.; J. Check students' work.

**Week 37, Day 2 (page 162)**
A. Check students' work. B. 13 + 9, 12 + 10, 11 + 11; C. $5.00; D. <, <, <, =; E. 36; F. 162; G. pie, 5, 3; H. pentagon; I. 160, 170, 180; J. 8 + 9 = 17

**Week 37, Day 3 (page 163)**
A. Check students' matches. B. 17; C. Add. Then, subtract. D. 3; E. Check students' work. F. 94; G. 70; H. two fifteen OR quarter past two; I. 517 < 561

**Week 37, Day 4 (page 164)**
A. 39 dishes; B. 656 = 50, 305 = 5, 599 = 500, 150 = 50; C. 8; D. 20; E. 13 – 9, 12 – 8, 11 – 7; F. 130; G. 328; H. 2 children; I. 2 in; J. 832, 75, 320

**Week 38, Day 1 (page 165)**
A. 6 books; B. 450; C. 20; D.Check students' work. E. 1 hundreds block and 6 ones blocks; F. Juan, Shamiah, Britney and Allen; G. 439; H. 630; I. 6:35; J. Check students' work.

**Week 38, Day 2 (page 166)**
A. 24 bibs; B. Clockwise from top: 9, 12, 9, 8, 10, 11, 15, 13, 14, 7; C. Check students' work. D. 5 + 12 = 17, 12 + 5 = 17, 17 – 5 = 12, 17 – 12 = 5; E. 73; F. 3 hundreds, 4 tens, 4 ones; G. 70 cm, 65 cm; H. 28 feet; I. 350, 360, 370; J. 73

**Week 38, Day 3 (page 167)**
A. Check students' work. B. 65 strawberries; C. 1, 9, 12; D. 2 hundreds, 6 tens; E. Check students' work. F. 53 – 11 = 42; G. sphere, rectangular prism, cone, cylinder; H. 11; I. 12, 9

**Week 38, Day 4 (page 168)**
A. 32, 29, 65; B. 4 tens; C. 600 + 60 + 3; D. 2, 1; E. Check students' work. F. 689; G. 732; H. 23 books; I. 1 meter; J. 77

**Week 39, Day 1 (page 169)**
A. 19; B. 614; C. 16; D. Check students' work. E. Check students' work. F. Check students' work. G. Check students' work. H. 210; I. 60¢; J. 12 in.

**Week 39, Day 2 (page 170)**
A. Check students' work. B. 3 + 3 = 6; C. 72; D. >, >, <, >; E. 634; F. 76; G. meterstick; H. two hundred ninety-two; I. 898; J. 18

**Week 39, Day 3 (page 171)**
A. 4 in; B. Check students' work. C. Add. Then, subtract; D. 11; E. trapezoid; F. 46 + 46 = 92; G. 90; H. 59; I. 416 < 461

**Week 39, Day 4 (page 172)**
A. 21 + 63 = 84, 44 + 32 = 76, 21 + 58 = 79; B. 20; C. 7; D. Check students' work. E. Check students' work. F. 24; G. hexagon; H. 15 cm; I. Check students' work. J. 778, 121

**Week 40, Day 1 (page 173)**
A. 14; B. From top to bottom: 13, 6, 10, 9, 19; C. 7; D. 3 cm; E. 781; F. Check students' work. G. 6:55; H. 20; I. $1.55; J. 292 < 392, 890 > 819, 551 > 155, 880 = 880, 992 > 929, 365 < 536

# Answer Key

**Week 40, Day 2 (page 174)**
A. Check students' work. B. From top to bottom:
27, 10, 17, 4, 11, 5; C. 81; D. >, =, >, <; E.
383; F. 143; G. 9, 5, running; H. From top to
bottom: 54, 56, 65, 66, 75, 76; I. 335;
J. 13, 19

**Week 40, Day 3 (page 175)**
A. 2 in., 5 cm; B. 103¢; C. Check students' work.
D. 8; E. 2 + 2 + 2 + 2 = 8; F. 88 − 52 = 36;
G. pyramid; H. 3 hundreds, 3 tens, 5 ones; I. 17,
14

**Week 40, Day 4 (page 176)**
A. 457, 58, 575; B. 12 olives; C. 319, 317, 313,
311; D. even; E. 361; F. 2; G. 859; H. 3 in; I. 9
+ 9 = 18; J. 300 + 50 + 5, 500 + 30 + 3

# Notes